# The Rainbow of Faiths

# The Rainbow
# of Faiths

*Critical Dialogues on Religious Pluralism*

John Hick

SCM PRESS LTD

0 334 02608 3

First published 1995
by SCM Press Ltd
9–17 St Albans Place,
London N1 0NX

Typeset at The Spartan Press Ltd,
Lymington, Hants
and printed in Great Britain by
Mackays of Chatham PLC, Chatham, Kent

Dedicated to
Hazel

# Contents

# Contents

# Preface

At the end of the twentieth century Christianity is in deep crisis. The theological structure developed by the Western church has come to seem hollow and irrelevant to the majority of Westerners, and seems foreign and alien, as an extension of Western cultural hegemony, to many Christians in Africa, India, China, and the East generally.

There are several aspects to this crisis, and this book is concerned with one of them – the widespread realization that Christianity is only one among several great world religions. Judaism, Islam, Hinduism, Buddhism now appear to many as different but, judging by their fruits in human life, equally authentic responses to God, the Divine, the Ultimate, the Real. This (often implicit rather than explicit) acceptance of religious pluralism carries with it a need to rethink the dogmas that imply Christianity's religious superiority not only for those of us who have been formed by it but for the entire human race. When this is done, an intellectually honest and realistic Christian faith may yet be able to speak to the deep religious concern that exists as strongly as ever among a Western population that has long since ceased to be captivated by traditional institutional religion.

There is a range of understandings of religious pluralism, and in the 1994 Auburn Lectures at Union Theological Seminary, New York, I was asked to respond to criticisms of the version that I have advocated. This sees the great world faiths as very different but (so far as we can tell) equally valid ways of conceiving, experiencing, and responding in life to the ultimate reality that we call God. The rainbow, as the sun's light refracted by the earth's atmosphere into a glorious spectrum of colours, is a metaphor for the refraction of the divine Light by our human religious cultures. This conception has been welcomed by some but strongly criticized by others, and what follows is an attempt to answer the criticisms, largely in the form of a dialogue with a philosopher, Phil, and a theologian, Grace.

A number of thanks and some further explanations are in order, but I have placed them in Appendix I for the convenience of readers who prefer at this point to get straight into the argument.

John Hick, February 1995

**Institute for Advanced Research in the Humanities,
University of Birmingham, UK**

# Introduction

# On Theological Controversy

The fact that there is a plurality of great world religions is experienced today by many Christians as both a practical and an intellectual problem. This book is concerned primarily with the intellectual problem as this is being addressed by theologians and philosophers.

We have to begin by recognizing that almost every topic in these two fields, philosophy and theology, is controversial. Indeed this has always been the case, although for many centuries theological discussion, in particular, was monitored and restricted by a dominant orthodoxy allied with secular power. This was the case roughly from the Council of Chalcedon in 451 CE to the Reformation in the sixteenth century, and then separately within Catholicism and Protestantism until the eighteenth century. More recently diversity of views, debate, disagreement have flourished relatively freely. I say 'relatively' because under the papacy of John Paul II there have been strong institutional pressures upon Catholic theologians to adhere to Vatican teaching, particularly on moral questions; and in the Baptist, Presbyterian, and Methodist churches in the USA there has for several years been a shift to the right, with theological questioning and experiment institutionally discouraged; whilst on the other side of the Atlantic a Church of England priest was recently dismissed from his post for expressing ultra-liberal views – the first time this has happened for several generations. So the official structures of the mainline churches are not today particularly hospitable to controversial ideas. However, 'heretics' and 'radicals' are no longer burned at the stake or tortured by the Inquisition. Anything can now be said, even though sometimes at a cost to the career prospects of the one who says it.

But on the other hand whilst the churches present this mixed picture of free debate and enforced orthodoxy, the academic world is a much more open field for the testing of ideas in vigorous controversy. In the USA this results in uninhibited debate about virtually everything. In Britain, theological diversity is still residually restricted by the fact that some of the most prestigious English university chairs are reserved by law for ordained clergy of the Anglican Church, and that the Church of Scotland still has a considerable say in appointments to Scottish theological chairs. And there is a like or greater restrictive ecclesiastical influence in both Catholic and Protestant senior academic appointments in the German universities.

However, despite these limiting factors a great deal of good discussion and debate does take place, and it is through this that issues are gradually clarified and a degree of consensus sometimes reached.

This occurs in many different contexts – informal discussion between colleagues in a university or college or seminary department; organized local discussion groups and seminars; questions, comments, and responses after public lectures and after papers read at conferences; and in journal articles and reviews, and of course in books.

The aim of theological and philosophical dialogue is not necessarily to come to an agreement – though this of course is much to be desired, and sometimes happens – but to locate the differences more precisely and to see what the pros and cons of a question are. But my impression as one who has been involved in these different types of discussion and argument for a number of years is that we – the academic community – do not generally conduct our controversies very well.

The main reason consists, I think, in the sheer practical difficulties of effective communication within such a large and diffused set of individuals. If two philosophers or theologians, who are reasonable and civilized people, get together for long enough to discuss a specific question they can get to the point at which each sees clearly what the other's position is and what the other's arguments for it are (so as to be able to report them accurately to a third party), and at which each has identified his or her own and the other's presuppositions. At this point either one has been converted to the other's view of the matter, or they jointly construct something new which is different from the initial position of either, or they agree to differ, knowing clearly what they are disagreeing about.

But this does not happen very often. Life is too busy in today's universities and colleges for it to be easy to have long, unhurried discussions. Particularly in the USA, people in different universities live at great distances from one another, so that personal meetings tend to occur mainly at conferences and conventions. A potentially important new factor is the development of e-mail networks of scholars interested in particular topics. But e-mail dialogue actually takes longer than face to face discussion, and it is not yet clear to what extent these networks are going to transform the situation. They must be a considerable help within certain limited groups but will not solve the large-scale problem.

E-mail apart, what usually happens is this. You read a paper at a conference, and fellow academics in the audience ask questions or make critical points. Sometimes a clear question or remark can receive a clear response. Sometimes a question is a verbal missile rather than a serious point and one has to try to evade or explode or toss it back as best one can. Sometimes a question is really a complex volley of only loosely related questions and remarks, or both, and it is impossible to take the time to respond properly to all of them in view of the fact that others want to ask their own questions – and often there is half an hour or less available for the discussion part of the session; so one picks out of the volley something that can be answered quickly. But sometimes of course a really good critical point is raised and leads to a really productive discussion. In general, however, this familiar format, although probably the best that can be devised for conference sessions, provides an opportunity for the paper reader to express his or her views, and for a few scattered critical responses to be heard, but is not an occasion for prolonged and focussed discussion. It sometimes gets nearer to this when there are prepared responses by one or two people who are on the program and have received the paper well in advance. But it may require them all to go off afterwards for a meal or a drink together to continue the argument to the point of full clarification – and often in a busy conference day this is not easy.

Or again, you publish a journal article, or a book, and if it is sufficiently interesting some other scholars write articles discussing it. Such critical articles may motivate you to respond to them. Sometimes you do so, not because the article makes a significant point, but because you think it has badly misrepresented you and you want to set the record straight. But more often the critic makes legitimate points, to which you respond, and there may be some useful long-distance discussion – though usually not as productive as it would be if you could meet face to face. And if there are a number of articles you may well not want to take the time to respond to them all. (If I had responded to every critical article about my own work, on the epistemology of religion, theodicy, eschatology, christology, and religious pluralism, I should have had to write about a hundred and thirty articles, the equivalent of perhaps twelve books – though this calculation is of course meaningless in that these twelve books would have been instead of the books that I have in fact written, which occasioned the critical articles!)

Again, discussion between books – you criticize someone else's views in a book of your own, and vice versa, – is generally even less satisfying than discussion in articles. For when you refer to another author you are often only citing one particular remark or argument, sometimes only one sentence; and the author quoted will very likely feel that you have not done justice to his or her thought as a whole – and will probably be justified in feeling this. Such references to others, or by others to oneself, are of course entirely in order; but they do not always or even usually amount to a productive dialogue.

The overall result is that the professional discussion of contentious issues is not in as good a state as we would all wish. It is a little like the confused medley of conversations in a crowded place, in which everyone speaks but no one hears clearly what the others are saying and no topic gets fully and properly discussed. The situation is better, generally speaking, among philosophers than among theologians because philosophical issues can often be more precisely defined; but even there it is far from ideal.

Book reviewing is another forum for critical responses. A good review tells the reader who the book is intended for, gives an accurate summary of what the author says, and then offers the reviewer's own critical comments and a balanced assessment of the interest and value of the work. Such a review can be extremely helpful to readers who have to decide what to read among the plethora of new books in their field each year. It can also be helpful to the author, for he or she knows that the reviewer has studied the book with great care. But all too often reviews are not like this. All too often they fail to give any accurate account of what the book says, but merely give vent to the reviewer's opinions on the subject generally. They fail to realize that one is not offered a book to review primarily in order to sit in judgment upon it, but primarily to write a critical – in the sense of a knowledgeable and thoughtful – introduction of it to readers of the journal, and sometimes to begin a debate about it. Bad reviewing can however be discouraged, and could indeed be largely eliminated, if journal editors would insist upon a responsible code of practice for their reviewers.

Nevertheless, these are the forms of communication that we have – apart from the sometimes very productive and satisfying one to one and small group discussions which, however, seem increasingly difficult to arrange as the administrative overload of academic life increases. And so the practical question is whether we can do anything to improve our communication procedures in the journals and books. Here I suggest a few rather obvious points in the etiquette and ethics of controversy – addressed to myself as much as to anyone else.

First, when you criticize someone's, say an imaginary Mary Smith's, views you should establish your right to do so by summarizing her position accurately, even if pressure of space means that you can only do so briefly. From Mary's point of view it is very satisfying to know that a colleague in the academic world has taken the trouble to read carefully what she has written. And from the point of view of readers of the journal it shows that you are not expressing a mere knee-jerk reaction after a rapid scan of the book but have assimilated it and are in a position to make serious and considered criticisms. On the other hand it is irritating to have one's views misrepresented in print, because you know that there will unfortunately be people who read the criticism without bothering to read you.

Secondly, it does not help to be rude, even though this may be therapeutic for yourself. So be as venomous as you like in your first draft, but cut out the cutting sarcasm, expunge the contemptuous expression, snip out the snide comment, obliterate the bitter retort before you publish. This may be a painful sacrifice; but do you really want to foul up the precious channels of communication? A face to face discussion is not likely to be productive once the participants have started to abuse one another, and neither is discussion in a learned (or indeed in a popular) journal.

Thirdly, it is not fair to select one of Mary Smith's paragraphs and complain that she has not said in it something that is not relevant at that particular point, and doubly unfair if she has said it somewhere else, where it was relevant.

Fourthly, we should always remember, when getting polemical, that there is likely to be some truth even in a position that we reject. No serious and competent thinker is likely to be *completely* wrong. He or she is probably looking at the same data, but from a significantly different angle, or is selecting a partly different set of data because of different presuppositions. But even so, there still are likely to be a number of relevant matters on which you think alike. Contrary positions are not always as contrary as their protagonists think, and it can help to pinpoint the differences if you first list the points of agreement.

I have been speaking mainly about debates within the academic world. But of course the same principles apply to all intelligent discussion wherever it occurs, including church groups, adult education courses, lay conferences, talk in pubs and clubs and at dinner parties and in any other forum.

However, even when all these principles are observed,[1] there

----

[1] One other thing to avoid is happily rare enough to rate only a footnote. If Mary Smith has been writing over a number of years, during which she has developed her views and now says some things that are inconsistent with what she said a decade or so ago, it is grossly unfair to bring together an earlier and a later statement and present them as a single self-contradictory position. I mention this misdemeanour because I have myself been a victim of it.

is a basic and unavoidable further factor which affects all discussion of issues like that treated in this book. Suppose two Christians are talking together about one of the issues that is central to our topic. One of them believes that Jesus was God (in the sense of being one of three persons of a divine Trinity) incarnate, and thus the uniquely full and final revelation of the divine for all humankind. The other believes that Jesus was a man who was remarkably open and responsive to the divine presence, who impressively lived out his own teachings concerning God's love and how to live in God's world, and whom we have accepted as our spiritual leader and guide. They will back up their convictions with arguments about whether Jesus really said this or that, about how much it matters whether or not he said it, about the historical reliability of the various New Testament documents, about the extent to which the development of Christian doctrine has been divinely guided, about the possibility of making sense of the orthodox two-natures idea, about whether it matters whether you can make sense of it or not, about the goods and evils of Christian civilization through the centuries, and so on. Both may think that they have established their cases. But normally each is so committed to their positions that if some of their arguments come to seem untenable this does not faze them: they simply go home and think up new arguments! For our beliefs in this area or in any other fundamental area are global conclusions arising from a vast array of influences and considerations – the family and culture and epoch into which we were born, our education and life experiences, our reading and interaction with others, our encounters with spiritually impressive individuals, etc. etc. Much more goes into it than clearly articulated arguments, and indeed our deepest convictions do not usually really depend upon the arguments that we produce to defend them.

This is very obvious at the fundamental level of our adherence to our own religion rather than another. Is it because of carefully weighed arguments that I am a Christian rather than a Muslim or a Buddhist? Does it not rather have a great deal to do with the fact that I was born in England rather than, say, in Saudi Arabia or Thailand, so that when the moment of religious awakening came the experience took a Christian rather than a Muslim or a Buddhist form? Of course if I had been born in either of these other countries, it would not have been the same I, because we are so largely formed by our culture. So the point has to be put differently. When someone, anyone, is born to Muslim parents in Egypt or Pakistan or Indonesia that person is very likely to become a Muslim; when to Buddhist parents in Tibet or Sri Lanka or Japan, to become a Buddhist; when to Hindu parents in India, to become a Hindu; when to Christian parents in Mexico or Poland or Italy to become a Catholic Christian; and so on. The religion creates us in its own image, so that naturally it fits us and we fit it as no other can.[2] And having been thus formed by one of these traditions it seems obvious to us that it is right/true/ normative/superior to all others. But this obviousness does not usually depend upon evidences and arguments, nor will it easily be swayed by contrary evidences and arguments.

It seems likely that in the largely post-Christian West we are now entering a new era in which young people are no longer so strongly formed by a tradition as to take its truth for granted. And yet there continues to be a high level of interest, most of it outside the churches, in the deep questions of the meaning of our existence. It may be that many will examine the different religious options and make their own choice, some being attracted to Christianity, some to Buddhism, some to Islam, some to Hinduism, and so on, and some by an eclectic spiritu-

---

[2]This thought has been objected to by Julius Lipner, who thinks that it presupposes that 'the human self is some sort of noumenal entity, existent before birth or conception in a nondescript incorporeal state' ('Does Copernicus Help?', *Religious Studies*, Vol. 13, no. 2, June 1977, p. 255.) But why should it presuppose this? I cannot think of any reason. And Roger Trigg has objected on the ground that it is equally true that someone brought up by atheist parents may well become an atheist, so that the relativity of belief to upbringing does not necessarily support a religious as distinguished from a naturalistic philosophy. ('Religion and the Threat of Relativism', *Religious Studies*, Vol. 19, no. 3, September 1983, p. 298). But of course it is not intended to do that. It is intended to remind religious people of the correlation between their specific beliefs and the circumstances of their birth and upbringing, as a hint to treat those specific beliefs with a 'hermeneutics of suspicion'.

ality that draws upon a variety of sources. But this is a new situation and we have yet to see how it will develop in the twenty-first century.

Within a given tradition theological choices are generally less fundamental. But of course the range of permissible options is itself an important matter of judgment and conviction; and this is no less the case if one decides to believe what one's church teaches, for this decision already presupposes a judgment about the divine authority of the church. The particular case of the deity of Jesus qualifies as fundamental for many Christians. Since the Council of Nicea in 312 CE, when the belief was officially adopted, the leaders of institutional Christianity have defined this as the central Christian belief. And yet today there are many Christian theologians and lay men and women who accept it in very qualified senses – as a metaphorical statement, or in terms of degrees of divinity, or as a traditional formula whose implications (and thus a large part of whose meaning) they tacitly ignore. From the point of view of the church leadership this is disbelief. From the point of view of the growing number of church members who have moved in this direction it constitutes a greater realism and honesty. But on this issue the orthodox and the heterodox, or traditionalist and progressive, have significantly different global judgments, which are attacked and defended with arguments that however do not usually reach the deeper sources of belief. Changes of mind can and do occur as a result of a lengthy mulling over of the matter in a wide perspective, but not generally as a result of specific knock-down arguments.

And so the aim of this book is to feed such long-term reflection. I hope in the course of it to correct some misapprehensions, to clarify some issues, to show why a Christian pluralism is permissible and why it is attractive to a growing number of people both inside and outside the churches. The criticisms of the pluralist point of view that I discuss have been formulated by theologians and philosophers; but the issues are equally the concern of thoughtful men and women who are not professional theologians or philosophers. And so this book is intended for anyone who would welcome some stimulus and some guidelines in thinking for themselves about what is today a great thorny question both for Christians and for people of different faiths.

# I

# The Pluralistic Hypothesis

May I say first that I feel highly honoured to have been invited to give this first series of Auburn Lectures, and to give them on a subject which has for some years now been rising on the theological and practical agenda of the churches, namely the relation between Christians and people of different faiths. The subject is a controversial one. Indeed everything of real interest in theology today is controversial, and if the church as a whole is not to descend into bitter argument and mutual anathematizing we have to become accustomed to the rich internal diversity of Christian thought. I realize, however, that what I'm going to say can only appear as an undermining of faith, as heresy or apostacy, to many at the more conservative end of the Christian spectrum. It's also true that some of the positions taken by very conservative Christians on this issue strike others of us as no longer tenable. But we nevertheless have to be willing to listen to one another, hopefully with human courtesy and Christian charity. I hope therefore to try, as a contribution to the ongoing debates, to give reasons for my proposals rather than simply assert them, and specific arguments against ideas that seem to me to be mistaken rather than simply rejecting them out of hand.

## Starting at ground level

By different faiths from our own I shall have in mind primarily the other 'great world religions', and specifically Judaism, Islam, Hinduism and Buddhism. This is not because other smaller and other newer religions, as well as 'primal' religion, and the great secular faiths of Humanism and Marxism, are not in themselves of equal intrinsic importance, but merely because time is limited and because what are generally called the great world faiths have been in existence for many centuries, affecting many millions of people, so that enough is publicly known about them for it to be possible to discuss them against a common background of knowledge. I would, however, like to stress the phrase '*people* of different faiths', because I am going to suggest that the way forward in this perplexing area is to be found by looking first at the actual lives of people within the contexts of our own and other traditions.

From this ground level starting point I shall move towards what I regard as an appropriate Christian theology of religions for today. I say 'for today' because theology is a growing and developing organism, so that an appropriate theological framework for today and tomorrow may well differ from what was appropriate a thousand years ago or indeed, as the pace of cultural change has increased, a hundred years ago or even a generation ago.

The new conditions affecting our understanding of the world religions have been gradually forming during the last three centuries. During what is called the European Enlightenment of the seventeenth and eighteenth centuries there developed a Western realization that Christendom is part of a much larger human world, with great civilizations having existed outside it, above all in China and India as well as the Islamic world; and along with this the realization that Christianity is one world religion amongst others. It was then that the generic idea of religion became established in educated circles, with Christianity seen as one particular form. But now, and particularly since the end of the Second World War, this awareness has become prominent in public consciousness. At least three developments have contributed to this. One has been an explosion of information in the West about the religions of the world. First rate scholarship, published in reasonably cheap paperbacks, is now readily available concerning – taking them in order of antiquity – Hinduism, Judaism, Buddhism, Jainism, Taoism, Confucianism, Islam, Sikhism, Baha'i, as well as the primal or indigenous religions of Africa, North and South America, Australasia, and elsewhere. Secondly, travel opportunities have multiplied and great numbers of Westerners have spent time in India, Turkey, Egypt, Thailand, Sri Lanka and other non-Christian countries, and have seen something of the peaceful influence of Buddhism among the Thai people, something of the ecstatic devotion and the powerful sense of the divine among Hindus, something of the marvels of Islamic civilization as expressed architecturally in, for example, the Taj Mahal at Agra or the great mosques of Istanbul; and many Westerners have also made their own mind-expanding and consciousness-altering inner journeys in the practice of Eastern methods of meditation. And third, and perhaps most important of all, there has been massive immigration from East to West, bringing Muslims, Sikhs, Hindus, Buddhists to settle in Europe and North America. There are, for example, between four and five million Muslims in North America, and about five million in Europe; and there are also in the West smaller but still quite large numbers of Hindus, Sikhs, and Buddhists, as well of course as the long-established Jewish communities, tragically reduced by a third in the Nazi Holocaust of the 1940s. As a result of this post-war immigration we are now familiar in many major cities of the Western world – including my own city of Birmingham, England – not only with churches and synagogues but also with mosques, gurudwaras, meditation centres, and temples of many kinds; and may have worshippers in these places as neighbours.

A further result, making an even deeper and more significant impression on many people is the fact that by coming to know individuals and families of these various faiths it has become a fairly common discovery that our Muslim or Jewish or Hindu or Sikh or Buddhist fellow citizens are in general no less kindly, honest, thoughtful for others, no less truthful, honourable, loving and compassionate, than are in general our Christian fellow citizens. People of other faiths are not on average noticeably better human beings than Christians, but nor on the other hand are they on average noticeably worse human beings. We find that both the virtues and the vices are, so far as we can tell, more or less equally spread among the population, of whatever major faith – and here I include Humanism and Marxism as major (though secular rather than religious) faiths. At any rate I have to record the fact that my own inevitably limited experience of knowing people who are Jews, Muslims, Hindus and Buddhists, including a few remarkable individuals of these religions as well as more ordinary individuals and families, both in the United States and Europe and also in India, Africa, Sri Lanka, and Japan, has led me to think that the spiritual and moral fruits of these faiths, although different, are more or less on a par with the fruits of Christianity; and reading some of the literature of the different traditions, both some of their scriptures and philosophies and also some of their novels and poetry portraying ordinary life, has reinforced this impression.

And again, when we look at the great civilizations of the earth, informed as they have been by different religious faiths, we see both great goods and great evils in each. But it doesn't seem possible to make a comparative assessment of these goods and evils in any acceptable way so as to establish the moral superiority of Christian civilization. For the goods and evils are so often incommensurate. How do you weigh the evils of the Indian caste system over the centuries against the evils of the European class system over the same centuries; or the poverty of so many Buddhist, Hindu and Muslim countries against the greedy use of the earth's non-renewable resources and the selfish destruction of the environment by so many Christian countries; or the social problems of Calcutta or Bangkok or Cairo against the poverty, drugs, violence, crime and despair in many of our own inner cities; or the cruelties of some Eastern regimes against the virulent anti-Semitism of Christian Europe? It is easy, of course, to pick out some manifest evil within another tradition and compare it with some manifest good within one's own. But this is not a truthful way of proceeding. The fact is that for every evil that you can quite rightly point to in another strand of history, it is possible with equal justification to point to a different but more or less equally reprehensible feature of one's own. We have to see the world religions as vast complex religio-cultural totalities, each a bewildering mixture of varied goods and evils. And when we do so we find that we have no way of objectively calibrating their respective values, adding so many points for this feature and deducting so many for that. We can, I suggest, only come to the negative conclusion that it is not possible to establish the unique moral superiority of any one of the great world faiths. It may be that in the sight of God one of them has in fact been, as an historical reality, superior to the others, but I don't think that from our human point of view we can claim to know this.

This conclusion, although a modest one, is in fact extremely significant for the argument that I want to develop. However, even this modest and negative judgment won't be acceptable to everyone. There are, I'm sure, many who are convinced that the fruits of Christian faith, in the lives of Christians and in the history of Christian civilization, are demonstrably superior to those of any other of the great world religions; and it's worth asking whether they believe that they can establish this conviction empirically, in terms of historical and sociological data, or whether it is an *a priori* claim which doesn't need to be supported by evidence? I would only say that the onus of proof lies squarely upon anyone who claims that the fruits in human life of his or her own religion are manifestly superior to those of all others. But for the moment I shall proceed on the basis that the traditional assumption of Christian moral pre-eminence, although deeply-rooted, cannot in fact be substantiated.

The bearing of this upon a Christian theology of religions is that the lack of observable moral superiority is at variance with our traditional theology. Our traditional theology tells us that Jesus of Nazareth was God – more precisely, God the Son, the second person of the Holy Trinity – incarnate, that he died on the cross to atone for the sins of the world, thus making salvation possible, that he founded the Christian church to proclaim this to the ends of the earth, and that Christians, as members of the Body of Christ, are indwelt by the Holy Spirit and spiritually fed week by week by divine grace in the eucharist. One implication of this is that Christianity, alone among the religions, was founded by God in person. It is thus God's own religion in a sense in which no other can be. Must God not then wish all human beings to enter the religion that God has come down from heaven to earth to provide? A second implication is that those of us who are part of it, a part of the Body of Christ, live in a closer relationship with God than those outside it. Ought there not then to be more evidence in Christian lives than in the lives of others of those fruits of the Spirit which St Paul listed as 'love, joy, peace, patience, kindness, goodness, faithfulness, gentleness, self-control' (Gal. 5.22–3)? If our traditional Christian theology is true, surely we should expect these fruits to be present more fully in Christians generally than in non-Christians generally. One cannot of course say that any randomly chosen Christian should be expected to be morally and spiritually superior to any randomly chosen non-Christian. That would be an unreasonable demand. But surely the *average* level of these fruits should be higher among Christians than among non-Christians. 'You will know them by their fruits', said Jesus, asking 'Are grapes gathered from thorns, or figs from thistles?' (Matt. 7.16). But I have been suggesting that, so far as we can tell, these visible fruits do *not* occur more abundantly among Christians than among Jews, Muslims, Hindus, Buddhists, Sikhs, Taoists, Baha'is, and so on. And yet surely they ought to if the situation were as it is pictured in our traditional Christian theology. I am thus led to conclude that this theology is in need of revision. For surely it's function is to make sense of the facts, not to be a device for systematically ignoring or contradicting them.

## Salvation

Let's now look at the situation again from a slightly different angle. Let's concentrate on the idea of salvation, an idea that is absolutely central to Christian thought, both traditional and revisionary. If we define salvation as being forgiven and accepted by God because of the atoning death of Jesus, then it is a tautology that Christianity alone knows and teaches the saving truth that we must take Jesus as our lord and saviour, plead his atoning death, and enter into the church as the community of the redeemed, in which the fruits of the Spirit abound. But we've seen that this circle of ideas contradicts our observation that the fruits of the Spirit seem to be as much (and as little) evident outside the church as within it. I suggest that we should continue to follow the clue provided by these fruits; for Jesus was clearly more concerned with men's and women's lives than with any body of theological propositions that they might have in their minds.

Indeed in his parable of the sheep and the goats the criterion of divine judgment is simply whether we have fed the hungry, welcomed the stranger, clothed the naked, and visited the sick and the imprisoned (Matt. 25. 31–46) – in other words, whether our lives have shown the fruits of the Spirit. Suppose, then, we define salvation in a very concrete way, as an actual change in human beings, a change which can be identified – when it *can* be identified – by its moral fruits. We then find that we are talking about something that is of central concern to each of the great world faiths. Each in its different way calls us to transcend the ego point of view, which is the source of all selfishness, greed, exploitation, cruelty, and injustice, and to become re-centred in that ultimate mystery for which we, in our Christian language, use the term God. We are, in the words (transposed into inclusive language) of the *Theologia Germanica*, to be to the Eternal Goodness what our own hands are to ourselves.[1] In Muslim terms, we are to submit absolutely to God, doing God's will and finding in this the fulfilment of our humanity. In Jewish terms, we are to live with joy and responsibility in accordance with God's Torah, finding in this, once again, the fulfilment of our humanity. In Hindu terms, to quote Radhadkrishnan, 'The divine consciousness and will must become our consciousness and will. This means that our actual self must cease to be a private self; we must give up our particular will, die to our ego, by surrendering its whole nature, its consciousness and character to the Divine'.[2] And in Buddhist terms, to quote a leading contemporary exponent of Buddhism to the West, Masao Abe, 'Buddhist salvation is . . . nothing other than an awakening to reality through the death of the ego',[3] an awakening which expresses itself in compassion for all sentient life.

---

[1] *Theologia Germanica*, ch. 10, trans. Susanna Winkworth, London: Macmillan 1937, p. 32.

[2] S. Radhakrishnan, *The Principal Upanishads*, London: Allen & Unwin and New York: Humanities Press 1969, p. 105. Sir Sarvepalli Radhakrishnan was Professor of Eastern Religions and Ethics at Oxford University, and subsequently President of India, and was the author of a number of books on Eastern philosophy and religion.

[3] *The Buddha Eye*, ed. Frederick Franck, New York: Crossroad 1982, p. 153.

Without going further, it is I think clear that the great post-axial traditions, including Christianity, are directed towards a transformation of human existence from self-centredness to a re-centring in what in our inadequate human terms we speak of as God, or as Ultimate Reality, or the Transcendent, or the Real. Among these options I propose to use the term 'the Real', not because it is adequate – there is no adequate term – but because it is customary in Christian language to think of God as that which is alone finally real, and the term also corresponds to the Sanscrit *sat* and the Arabic *al-Haqq* and has parallels in yet other languages. And what is variously called salvation or liberation or enlightenment or awakening consists in this transformation from self-centredness to Reality-centredness. For brevity's sake, I'll use the hybrid term 'salvation/liberation'. I suggest that this is the central concern of all the great world religions. They are not primarily philosophies or theologies but primarily ways of salvation/liberation. And it is clear that salvation, in this sense of an actual change in human beings from natural self-centredness towards a recentring in the Divine, the Ultimate, the Real, is a long process – though there are often peak moments within it – and that this process is taking place not only within Christianity but also, and so far as we can tell to a more or less equal extent, within the other great traditions.

I can now introduce the familiar three-fold distinction within Christian theologies of religion as exclusivist, inclusivist, and pluralist.[4] There are of course many variations within each of these, but the three-fold classification itself, when applied to both truth-claims and salvation-claims, seems to cover the range of options. I sometimes hear people say that they do not fit into any of these three categories. I then ask them what their own theology of religions is, and invariably it turns out either that they don't

---

[4] This widely used typology first appeared in print in Alan Race's *Christians and Religious Pluralism* (London: SCM Press and Maryknoll, New York, 1983, 2nd ed. 1994). It has recently been criticized by Ian Markham in 'Creating Options: Shattering the "Exclusivist, Inclusivist, and Pluralist" Paradigm', and defended by Gavin D'Costa in 'Creating Confusion: A Response to Markham', both in *New Blackfriars* (January 1993).

have one, so that naturally it does not exemplify any of the three types, or else they *do* have one and it is manifestly a variation of one or other of the three! You can of course double the number of options by adding the qualifier 'possibly' to each, as Schubert Ogden has done in the case of pluralism: he argues that as well as pluralism there is the view that pluralism is, from the Christian point of view, a theological possibility, a possibility which one may affirm without having to affirm that it is in fact realized.[5] This seems clearly right. But I don't think that it affects the basic three-fold distinction, and I shall accordingly continue to employ this widely used typology.

So let us speak first in terms of salvation claims. Here, exclusivism asserts that salvation is confined to Christians, or even more narrowly, in the traditional Catholic dogma, that *extra ecclesiam nulla salus*, outside the church there is no salvation. This exclusivist position was however implicitly repudiated by Vatican II, and again by the present Pope in his first encyclical, *Redemptor Hominis*, 1979, in which he said that 'man – every man without any exception whatever – has been redeemed by Christ, and . . . every man – with each man without any exception whatever – Christ is in a way united, even when man is unaware of it' (para. 14). The only salvation-exclusivists left are the few Catholic ultra-conservative followers of the late Archbishop Lefebvre, who was excommunicated in 1988, and a much more numerous, vociferous and influential body of Protestant fundamentalists. Their position is a consistent and coherent one for those who can believe that God condemns the majority of the human race, who have never encountered or who have not accepted the Christian gospel, to eternal damnation. Personally, I would view such a God as the Devil! But, more fundamentally, if we mean by salvation an actual salvific change in women and men, then it is, as I have been reminding us, an observable fact that this is not restricted either to any section of Christianity or to Christianity as a whole. Given this very concrete conception of salvation/libera-

---

[5]Schubert Ogden, *Is There Only One True Religion or Are There Many?*, Dallas: Southern Methodist University Press 1992.

tion, then, Christian exclusivism is not a live option, and I shall not now spend any more time on it.

The position taken by Vatican II, and by the Pope in the encyclical from which I just quoted, and also by the majority of both Catholic and Protestant theologians today other than many fundamentalists, is aptly called inclusivism. This acknowledges that the salvific process is taking place throughout the world, within each of the great world faiths and also outside them, but insists that wherever it occurs it is the work of Christ. Salvation, on this view, depends upon Jesus' atoning death on Calvary, though the benefits of that death are not confined to Christians but are available, in principle, to all human beings. Thus people of the other world faiths can be included within the sphere of Christian salvation. In Karl Rahner's famous phrase, they can be 'anonymous Christians'. Many inclusivists feel, understandably, uncomfortable with that imperialistic-sounding phrase; but their position is nevertheless essentially Rahner's – namely that salvation, whenever and wherever it occurs, is exclusively Christian salvation, so that Jews, Muslims, Hindus, Buddhists, and so on, who are saved are saved, and can only be saved, by Christ whether or not they know the source of their salvation.

This Christian inclusivism takes two forms. One defines salvation in traditional terms, holding that in order to be saved one must personally accept Jesus as one's lord and saviour, but adds that those who do not encounter him in this life may do so after death. This is an increasingly favoured option among conservative Christians who nevertheless cannot accept that God has ordained the eternal loss of the majority of humankind through no fault of their own. A recent Protestant example is Richard Swinburne in his *Responsibility and Atonement*,[6] and a recent Catholic example is Father J. A. DiNoia's 'Christian theology of religions in a prospective vein' in his *The Diversity of Religion*[7] – meaning by 'prospective' that non-Christians may receive salvation in or beyond death. My only comment upon this appeal to the life to come is that a theologian who insists upon the

---

[6]Oxford: Clarendon Press 1992, p. 173.
[7]Washington: Catholic University of America Press 1992, ch. 3.

unique superiority of Christianity but who cannot accept the exclusion of non-Christians as such from salvation, has no option but to take this step, even though it involves abandoning the traditional teaching that God's grace in Christ must be accepted in this present life and that death forecloses the options.[8] There should therefore be no concealment of the fact that one part of the dogmatic structure is being modified in order to retain the acceptability of another part and that this is being done, under the pressure of our modern sensibility, in order to make room for the salvation of the non-Christian majority of humankind. For those who define salvation in exclusively Christian terms some such doctrinal modification is today unavoidable. But it can also be dangerous to the long-term health of the dogma that is being saved. The new extension is analogous to the epicycles that were added to preserve the old Ptolemaic astronomy for a little longer before it finally collapsed. We should be warned that such theological epicycles tend to appear in the last days of a dying dogma!

The other form of inclusivism is compatible with the wider understanding of salvation as salvation/liberation, the actual transformation of men and women, and ultimately through them of societies, and can gladly acknowledge that this is happening – and happening in varying degrees now, in this life – outside Christianity as well as within it. It insists, however, that the salvific influences of the Torah in the lives of Jews, of Islam in the lives of Muslims, of Hindu spiritual practices in the lives of

---

[8]Thus St Augustine, affirming that unbaptized infants go to hell, says, 'If, therefore [after a string of biblical quotations], as so many and such divine witnesses agree, neither salvation nor eternal life can be hoped for by any man without baptism and the Lord's body and blood, it is vain to promise these blessings to infants without them', *On Forgiveness of Sins, and Baptism*, Book 1, ch. 34. (The Nicene and Post-Nicene Fathers, First Series, Vol. 5, ed. Philip Schaff, Grand Rapids, Michigan: Eerdmans 1956, p. 28.) The Council of Florence (1438–45) declared that everyone outside the church will go to hell 'unless before the end of life they are joined to the church' (*Denzinger*, 714). John Calvin wrote that 'the strange notion of those who think that unbelievers as to the coming of Christ, were after his death freed from their sin, needs no longer refutation; for it is an indubitable

Hindus, of the Buddhadharma in the lives of Buddhists, and so on, are all ultimately due to the salvific work of Christ, who is secretly at work within all these traditions. This is the idea of the unknown Christ of Hinduism – unknown, that is, to Hindus, – and likewise the unknown Christ of Buddhism, and so on. Here Christ has to mean, not the historical Jesus of Nazareth, but the resurrected Jesus in his divine glory, now thought of as the heavenly Christ. As a very general idea this sounds promising. However, the problem is to spell it out more precisely. It needs to be shown by what kind of invisible causality the saving death of Jesus around 30 CE has operated to make the other great religious traditions effective contexts of salvation/liberation, apparently to much the same extent as Christianity. It will not suffice to speak of the work of the resurrected Christ, since this presumably began with Jesus' resurrection around 30 CE – unless one is prepared to defend the idea of a causality operating backwards through time to account for the spiritually liberating power of the Buddha's teachings some five hundred years earlier, and indeed, to cover the beginnings of Hinduism and Judaism, operating backwards through time for more than a thousand years. This would, surely, be a philosophical quagmire that few would wish to get into.

In order to make sense of the idea of Christ at work within the world religions, including those that precede Christianity, it will be necessary to leave aside the historical figure of Jesus of Nazareth, and his death on the cross, and to speak instead of a non-historical, or supra-historical, Christ-figure or Logos (i.e. the second person of the Trinity) who secretly inspired the Buddha, and the writers of the Upanishads, and Moses and the great Hebrew prophets, and Confucius and Lao-Tze and Zoroaster before the common era , as well as Muhammad, Guru Nanak, Ramakrishna and many others since. But this Christ figure, or Logos, operating before and thus independently of the historical life and death of Jesus of Nazareth, then becomes in effect a name

---

doctrine of Scripture, that we obtain not salvation in Christ except by faith; then there is no hope left for those who continue to death unbelieving' (*Commentary on the Catholic Epistles*, trans. John Owen, Edinburgh: Calvin Society 1856, p. 113).

for the world-wide and history-long presence and impact upon human life of the Divine, the Transcendent, the Ultimate, the Real. In other words, in order to make sense of the idea that the great world religions are all inspired and made salvific by the same transcendent influence we have to go beyond the historical figure of Jesus to a universal source of all salvific transformation. Christians may call this the cosmic Christ or the eternal Logos; Hindus and Buddhists may call it the Dharma; Muslims may call it Allah; Taoists may call it the Tao; and so on. But what we then have is no longer (to put it paradoxically) an exclusively Christian inclusivism, but a plurality of mutually inclusive inclusivisms which is close to the kind of pluralism that I want to recommend. I am suggesting in effect that religious inclusivism is a vague conception which, when pressed to become clear, moves towards pluralism. I will try presently to indicate what such a pluralism involves.

## Truth-claims

But first let's return to something I pointed out earlier, namely that the three-fold exclusivism, inclusivism, pluralism scheme can be applied both to salvation-claims and also to truth-claims. Thus far we've been looking at it in terms of salvation-claims. But what about truth-claims? For it's undoubtedly the case that the great world faiths have developed very different belief-systems. According to some, the ultimate is personal, according to others non-personal. Among those which speak of a personal God, Christianity teaches that the one and only God is triune and that Jesus of Nazareth was the second person of this Trinity living a human life; whilst Judaism teaches that the one and only God is not triune but strictly unitary, and has selected the Jewish race as God's chosen people and frequently intervened in their history in Palestine, Egypt, and Babylonia; whilst Islam teaches that the one and only God is unitary but is directly self-revealed in the Qur'an, and has intervened in the life of the Muslim community in Mecca and Medina. Again, Vaishnavite Hinduism believes in the personal Vishnu, who has become incarnate in Krishna and in a number of other earthly figures; and Saivite Hinduism believes in the divine lord Shiva, whose cosmic dance is the life of the universe. And so on. Again, among the non-theistic traditions, advaitic Hinduism speaks of the universal consciousness of Brahman, which in the depths of our being we all are; whilst different strands of Buddhism speak of the universal Buddha nature, or of the Dharmakaya, or Nirvana, or Sunyata; and Taoism of the eternal Tao whose nature cannot be spoken in human terms. There are thus many different conceptions of the Ultimate, the Real, related to correspondingly different forms of religious experience and, arising from these, correspondingly different belief-systems. But if any one of these belief-systems is true, in the sense of reflecting reality, must not all the others be false, at least in so far as they differ from it? As Bertrand Russell wrote, 'It is evident as a matter of logic that, since [the great world religions] disagree, not more than one of them can be true'.⁹ And yet I now want to question this basic assumption that there can be at most one true religion, in the sense of a religion teaching saving truth about the Ultimate and our relationship to the Ultimate. I want to suggest a different approach altogether, and shall do so by means of a series of three analogies.

Consider, first, the psychologist Jastrow's famous ambiguous duck-rabbit picture which Wittgenstein used in his discussion of seeing-as in the *Philosophical Investigations*.

Suppose there is a culture in which ducks are a familiar sight but rabbits are completely unknown and have never even been heard of; and another culture in which rabbits are familiar but ducks completely unknown. So when people in the duck-knowing

---

⁹Bertrand Russell, *Why I am Not a Christian*, London: Allen & Unwin 1957, p. xi.

culture see the ambiguous figure they naturally report that it's the picture of a duck. Indeed they may well claim to know that this is what it is; for lacking the concept of rabbit they are not aware that the picture is ambiguous. And of course the other way round with the rabbit-knowing culture. Here it's manifestly a rabbit and there is again no ambiguity about it. The people of these two cultures are fully entitled to affirm with full conviction that this is the picture of a duck, or of a rabbit, as the case may be. And each group, when told of another group who claim that the figure is something entirely different and alien to them, will maintain that that group are confused or mistaken in some perhaps inexplicable way.

But Wittgenstein would be able to offer an account of the situation according to which each group is right in what it affirms but wrong in its inference that the other group is mistaken. They are both, he could point out, right in virtue of the fact that what is actually there is capable of being equally correctly seen in two quite different ways, as a duck or as a rabbit.

The analogy that I am suggesting here is with the religious experience component of religion. And the possibility that I want to point to is that the ultimate ineffable Reality is capable of being authentically experienced in terms of different sets of human concepts, *as* Jahweh, *as* the Holy Trinity, *as* Allah, *as* Shiva, *as* Vishnu, and again *as* Brahman, *as* the Dharmakaya, *as* the Tao, and so on, these different personae and impersonae occurring at the interface between the Real and our differing religious mentalities and cultures.

A second analogy may help to suggest how this may be possible. This is the wave-particle complementarity in physics. It seems that if in an experimental situation you act upon light in one way, it is observed to have wave-like properties, and if in another way, to have particle-like properties. The properties it is observed to have depend upon how the observer acts in relation to it. As Ian Barbour writes, in describing Niels Bohr's complementarity principle, 'No sharp line can be drawn between the process of observation and what is observed';[10] and he quotes

---

[10] Ian Barbour, *Religion in an Age of Science*, Vol. I, London: SCM Press and New York: Harper & Row 1990, p. 98.

Henry Folse's interpretation of Bohr as implying an ontology which 'characterizes physical objects through their powers to appear in different phenomenal manifestations rather than through determinate properties corresponding to those of phenomenal objects as was held in the classical framework'.[11] The analogy that I have in mind here is with spiritual practices – prayer, forms of meditation, sacraments, common worship. In these practices we act in relation to the Real. The suggestion here is that if in the activity of I–Thou prayer we approach the Real as personal then we shall experience the Real as a personal deity. What we are then likely to be aware of will be a specific divine personality, involved in a particular strand of human history – the one who has chosen the Jewish people; or the heavenly Father of Jesus' teaching; or the divine being who spoke to the Arab peoples in the Qur'an, and so on. Or if our religious culture leads us to open ourselves to the Real in various forms of meditation, as the infinite non-personal being-consciousness-bliss of Brahman, or as the eternal Dharmakaya ever expressing itself in the limitless compassion of the Buddhas, then this is likely to be the way in which we shall experience the Real. Putting it in familar Christian language, revelation is a relational matter, taking different forms in relation to people whose religious receptivity has been formed by different traditions, with their different sets of concepts and their different kinds of spiritual practice.

A third analogy comes from cartography. Because the earth is a three-dimensional globe, any map of it on a two-dimensional surface must inevitably distort it, and there are different ways of systematically distorting it for different purposes, including for example the familiar cylindrical projection invented by Mercator which is used in constructing many of our maps of the world. But it does not follow that if one type of map is accurate the others must be inaccurate. If they are properly made, they are all accurate – and yet in another sense they are all inaccurate, in that they all inevitably distort. However, one may be more useful for

---

[11]Henry Folse, *The Philosophy of Niels Bohr: The Framework of Complementarity*, New York: North Holland 1985, p. 237, quoted by Barbour, op. cit., p. 99.

one purpose, another for another – for great circle navigating, for shorter journeys, for travel in the tropics, for travel nearer to the Poles, and so on. The analogy here is with theologies, both the different theologies of the same religion and the even more different theologies and philosophies of different religions. It could be that representations of the infinite divine reality in our finite human terms must be much *more* radically inadequate than a two-dimensional representation of the three-dimensional earth. And it could be that the conceptual maps drawn by the great traditions, although finite picturings of the Infinite, are all more or less equally reliable within their different projections, and more or less equally useful for guiding us on our journey through life. For our pilgrim's progress is our life-response to the Real. The great world faiths orient us in this journey, and in so far as they are, as we may say, in soteriological alignment with the Real, to follow their path will relate us rightly to the Real, opening us to what, in different conceptualites, we will call divine grace or supernatural enlightenment that will in turn bear visible fruit in our lives.

## The pluralist answer

The hypothesis to which these analogies point is that of an ultimate ineffable Reality which is the source and ground of everything, and which is such that in so far as the religious traditions are in soteriological alignment with it they are contexts of salvation/liberation. These traditions involve different human conceptions of the Real, with correspondingly different forms of experience of the Real, and correspondingly different forms of life in response to the Real.

But why suppose that the Real in itself is ineffable? By 'ineffable' I mean (with a qualification to be mentioned presently) having a nature that is beyond the scope of our networks of human concepts. Thus the Real in itself cannot properly be said to be personal or impersonal, purposive or non-purposive, good or evil, substance or process, even one or many. However, in denying, for example, that the Real is personal one is not thereby saying that it is impersonal, but rather that this conceptual

polarity or dualism does not apply. And the same with the other
dualisms. This does not, however, mean that the Real is to be
postulated as nothing, or a blank, but rather as a reality lying
outside the scope of our human conceptual systems. We cannot
describe it as it is in itself, but only as it is thought and experienced
in human terms – in traditional scholastic language, not *quoad se*
but always *quoad nos*. From within some traditions the Real is
known as personal and from within others as nonpersonal, and
from within all of them as being, from our human point of view,
good or benign or gracious, as the ground of all human
transformation from unhappy self-centredness to the blessedness
that is variously thought and experienced in this life as an eternal
quality of life/ as peace with God/ as nirvana/ as satori/ as moksha,
and beyond this life in ways beyond our present imagining.

Of course, as a relatively trivial point, to say that the Real is
ineffable is not to commit the logical indiscretion of saying that we
cannot characterize it at all, even in purely formal ways; for we
have already done so in saying that it is ineffable! It means that we
cannot properly attribute intrinsic qualities to it. But, again, this
does not mean that it is an empty blank; it means that its nature,
infinitely rich in itself, cannot be expressed in our human concepts.
Nor does it follow that we can say nothing significant about it. For
we can say that it is that which there must be if human religious
experience is not purely human projection but, whilst involving
projection, is at the same time a response to a transcendent Reality.
The difference between there being and there not being an ultimate
Reality which is variously conceived and experienced through the
'lenses' of the different religions is thus the difference between a
religious and a naturalistic interpretation of religion. If there were
only one religion, say Christianity, a religious interpretation of it
would naturally identify the Real with the Holy Trinity. But
because there are several world religions which seem to be
soteriologically more or less on a par, a religious interpretation of
religion cannot identify the Real with the intentional object of any
one of them to the exclusion of the others, and so has to resort to the
distinction between the Real as it is in itself and the Real as
variously thought and experienced within the different major
traditions.

This approach assumes the now very widespread view that what is perceived is always partly constructed by the perceiver. Our concepts enter into the formation of our awareness. The basic epistemological principle was enunciated long ago by Thomas Aquinas when he wrote that 'Things known are in the knower according to the mode of the knower'.[12] Now the mode of the religious knower is differently formed within the different traditions. Hence the different awarenesses of the Real around which these traditions have developed. In modern times it was Immanuel Kant who has argued most influentially that perception is not a passive registering of what is there but is always an active process of selecting, grouping, relating, extrapolating, and endowing with meaning by means of our human concepts. This led him to distinguish between the noumenal world, the world as it exists unperceived, and the phenomenal world, that same world as humanly perceived, with all the difference that the act of perception makes. I am suggesting applying this insight to our awareness of the Real, by distinguishing between the noumenal Real, the Real *an sich*, and the Real as humanly perceived in different ways as a range of divine phenomena.

Kant suggested that we are aware of our natural environment in terms of certain categories which the mind imposes in the formation of our conscious experience – for example, the categories of substance, or thinghood, and of causality. I am suggesting analogously that we are aware of our supernatural environment in terms of certain categories which the mind imposes in the formation of religious experience. The two basic religious categories are deity (the Real as personal) and the absolute (the Real as non-personal). Each of these categories is then made concrete, or in Kant's terminology 'schematized' – not, however, (as in his system) in terms of abstract time but in terms of the filled time of history and culture as the experienced Gods and Absolutes of the various religious traditions.

What difference does this hypothesis, in so far as it is adopted, make for religion as we know it? In one respect very little, in another quite a lot. If we are Christians, accepting our own

---

[12]*Summa Theologiae*, II/II, Q.1, art. 2.

tradition as one valid response among others to the Real, we should continue within it, living in relation to that 'face' of the Real that we know as the heavenly Father of Jesus' teaching – or, if we think of Christianity as a developed theological tradition, as the Holy Trinity of later church teaching. And hopefully one should have begun, in this nurturing context, to undergo the salvific transformation from natural self-centredness to a new orientation centred in God. And the same, of course, applies to the people of the other great world faiths. Each tradition will continue in its concrete particularity as its own unique response to the Real. As the sense of rivalry between them diminishes and they participate increasingly in inter-faith dialogue they will increasingly affect one another and each is likely to undergo change as a result, both influencing and being influenced by the others. But nevertheless within this growing interaction each will remain basically itself. In this respect, the pluralistic hypothesis makes comparatively little difference to the existing traditions. But in another respect it makes what is for some of them a major difference. For in coming to understand itself as one among several different valid human responses to the Real each will gradually de-emphasize that aspect of its teaching which entails its own unique superiority. Such an aspect has grown up within each tradition, though it is more central in some than in others. And to modify, and eventually abandon, this implicit or explicit claim to unique superiority will involve a theological development in each case. This will be easier for some traditions than others, and within each tradition easier for some individuals than others.

But the theological and other implications of this position will come out in the remaining lectures. These will not, however, be lectures in the ordinary sense, but dialogues with two characters whom I have constructed, Phil who is a philosopher and who will be presenting philosophical criticisms of religious pluralism, and Grace who is a theologian presenting theological criticisms.

# Post-Modernist and Other Critiques, and Conflicting Truth-Claims

**John:** Phil, I believe you're going to act as devil's advocate, presenting philosophical criticisms that have been made of religious pluralism.
**Phil:** Yes, devil's advocate, or perhaps God's advocate! This is something that our listeners will have to decide for themselves.
**John:** OK. Go ahead.

## Pluralism as Western intellectual imperialism

**Phil:** Well first of all, some see religious pluralism as a product of post-Enlightenment rationalism, and some who are influenced by Foucault, Derrida, Habermas, Levinas, and Adorno (although these writers themselves don't discuss this issue) link religious pluralism with a capitalist world hegemony which is concealed behind the current 'one world' idea. Actually there are several issues here, so suppose we take them one at a time?
**John:** Yes, good.
**Phil:** Well first of all, contemporary religious pluralism has arisen within and has been supported by a particular historical, social, and political context; and the post-modernists warn us to approach any such theory with a certain wariness to see if it conceals a hidden agenda of political or economic interest.
**John:** Yes, agreed. But let's hold on to common sense and not let the 'hermeneutic of suspicion' develop into a hermeneutic of paranoia! We ought not to rule out *a priori* the possibility that a comprehensive theory may be genuinely illuminating and worth adopting.

**Phil:**   Perhaps so; but now consider the particular context in which religious pluralism has emerged. The critics I have in mind see it as a child of the European Enlightenment of the seventeenth and eighteenth centuries, with its universalizing rationalism.[1] It was at this time that Westerners first began to think on a world scale and to consider religion generically, seeing the particular historical religions as its different forms. Kant, for example, held that 'There is only *one* (true) religion; but there can be *faiths* [i.e. creeds or 'ecclesiastical faiths'] of several kinds.'[2] That's the background. Now contemporary religious pluralism has arisen after the Second World War when the European colonial hegemony finally ended and when a general awareness came about, at least in the West, of the world as a single interdependent unity, with the images of 'one world' and 'the global village' becoming common. The pluralistic understanding of religion as a range of variations within our human awareness of the ultimately real is – these critics point out – of a piece with this growing sense of the underlying unity of the human family, which is itself a child of the European Enlightenment. Would you agree with this?

**John:**   Well, it's certainly true that during the Enlightenment period Western thought began, as you say, to expand its field of vision to the whole world. And clearly this is the historical background of contemporary Western religious pluralists. But it's also true that the idea of the world faiths as different responses to the same ultimate reality occurred centuries before the European Enlightenment and has also occurred outside the sphere of its influence, so that it cannot simply be attributed to it.

**Phil:**   I'll ask you to substantiate that presently. But first what about the linking of religious pluralism with the contemporary 'one world' idea ?

---

[1]E.g. John V. Apczynski, 'John Hick's Theocentrism: Revolutionary or Implictly Exclusivist?', *Modern Theology*, Vol. 8, no. 1 (January 1992), and Colin Gunton in Hugh Montefiore (ed.), *The Gospel and Contemporary Culture*, London: Mowbray 1992, pp. 86f.

[2]Immanuel Kant, *Religion Within the Limits of Reason Alone*, trans. Theodore Green and Hoyt Hudson, New York: Harper & Row 1960, p. 98.

**John:** Well, yes, there is an obvious linkage. The current development of religious pluralism has been made possible by this new global awareness, and also of course by the explosion of readily available information about the world religions. Modern knowledge about the integral character of the human story and the intertwinings of religious history has created an intellectual environment hospitable to religious pluralism. But so what? Surely this is no argument against religious pluralism. Would it be a valid argument against contemporary liberation theology that it was born in a situation of violent social injustice in South America? Or against contemporary feminist theology that it has arisen in a culture in which women are increasingly free to express themselves and to assert their rights? Surely not. New aspects of truth are coming to light all the time as new situations elicit them.

**Phil:** But you do agree, it seems, that for good or ill contemporary religious pluralism is the product of the current global tendency in human thought? Or indeed, as one critic suggests, of the naively idealistic enthusiasm of the 1960s?[3] Or even, as one critic suggests, that religious pluralism stems from the supermarket culture of our time: 'In a society which has exalted the autonomous individual as the supreme reality, we are accustomed to the rich variety offered on the supermarket shelves and to the freedom we have to choose our favourite brands. It is very natural that this mentality should pervade our view of religion. One may stick to one's favourite brand and acclaim its merits in song and praise; but to insist that everyone else should choose the same brand is unacceptable.'[4] How about this?

**John:** Well certainly the idealistic sixties, and the supermarkets, and also the homogenizing influence of TV, are aspects of the world in which religious pluralism has become prominent. But it would be fantastic to think – and probably no one does think – that it's simply a product of such factors. It's a product of all this

---

[3] Kieran Flanagan, 'Theological pluralism: A sociological critique', in Ian Hamnett (ed.), *Religious Pluralism and Unbelief*, London and New York, Routledge 1990, pp. 82–5.

[4] Lesslie Newbigin, *The Gospel in a Pluralist Society*, Grand Rapids, Michigan: Eerdmans and Geneva: WCC Publications 1989, p. 168.

together with a religious insight which is much more ancient and widespread. The central insight that the great world faiths are different responses to the one ultimate transcendent reality occurs, as I said a moment ago, both outside the influence of the European Enlightenment and also centuries before it – and long before the sixties culture in the US and Europe.

**Phil:**    For instance?

## Pre-modern religious pluralism

**John:**    Well, to begin with a contemporary non-Westerner, the Dalai Lama has said, 'I maintain that every major religion of the world – Buddhism, Christianity, Confucianism, Hinduism, Islam, Jainism, Judaism, Sikhism, Taoism, Zoroastrianism – has similar ideas of love, the same goal of benefiting humanity through spiritual practice, and the same effects of making their followers into better human beings . . . Differences of dogma may be ascribed to differences of time and circumstance as well as cultural influences'.[5] And going back a generation, the great Hindu social and political activist Mahatma Gandhi believed that religious pluralism was not only true but was a necessary basis for peace both in multi-religious India and in the multi-religious world. He said, 'No one faith is perfect. All faiths are equally dear to their respective votaries. What is wanted, therefore, is a living friendly contact among the followers of the great religions of the world and not a clash among them in the fruitless attempt on the part of each community to show the superiority of its faith over the rest . . . Hindus, Mussalmans, Christians, Parsis, Jews are convenient labels. But when I tear them down, I do not know which is which. We are all children of the same God.'[6]

**Phil:**    Yes, but of course both Gandhi and the Dalai Lama, although Easterners, nevertheless belong to our modern world and have been deeply influenced by it.

**John:**    Yes, true. But the Dalai Lama stands in the same tradi-

---

[5] The Dalai Lama, *A Human Approach to World Peace*, Boston: Wisdom Publications 1984, p. 13.

[6] M. K. Gandhi, *What Jesus Means to Me*, ed. R. K. Prabhu, Ahmedabad: Navajivan Publishing House 1959, pp. 23, 31.

tion as the Buddhist emperor Ashoka, in the third century CE, who instead of imposing his own faith on his empire, as was normal with rulers in the ancient world, sought to encourage all its religions equally and urged each to see what is good in the others. And behind Gandhi there stands a very ancient pluralistic religious outlook in India. The Vedas teach that 'The Real (*sat*) is one, but sages name it variously'.[7] And in the *Bhagavad Gita* the Lord Krishna says 'In whatsoever way men approach Me, in that same way do I accept them'.[8] Gandhiji was also influenced from his youth by the Jain teaching of *anekantavada*, the many-sidedness of truth. And going further back in Indian history we find a marvellously pluralistic outlook in north India in the fifteenth century. Guru Nanak, the founder of the Sikh tradition, began his prophetic career with a period of silence from which he emerged to proclaim that there are no Hindus and there are no Muslims, for all true worshippers of God are at one. And the Sikh scriptures, the *Adi Granth*, compiled later, includes not only the writings of the early Sikh gurus but also passages from Hindu and Muslim saints. One of the non-Sikhs included in it was Kabir, in the fifteenth century, who was equally revered by Muslims and Hindus. He taught that God is beyond all form but that the 'formless God takes a thousand forms in the eyes of His creatures'; and that 'Brahma suits His language to the understanding of His hearer'; and again, 'If God be within the mosque, then to whom does this world belong? If Ram be within the image that you find upon your pilgrimage, then who is there to know what happens without? Hari is in the East: Allah is in the West. Look within your heart, for there you will find both Karim and Ram; all the men and women of the world are His living forms.'[9]

**Phil:** Yes, though I notice that these are all from Hindu sources, at any rate in the broad sense in which Hindu just means of Indian origin.

---

[7] *Rig-Veda*, I, 164, 46.
[8] IV, 11, trans. Radhakrishnan.
[9] *Songs of Kabir*, translated by Rabindranath Tagore, New York: Samuel Weiser 1977, pp. 75, 92, 112.

**John:**   True. But earlier still, in the thirteenth and fourteenth centuries, the Sufis of Islam had taught that the divine light is refracted through many human lenses. Thus Ibn al-Arabi advised, 'Do not attach yourself to any particular creed exclusively, so that you disbelieve all the rest ... God, the omnipresent and omnipotent, is not limited to one creed, for He says, 'Wherever you turn, there is the face of Allah' (Qur'an, 2: 115)'.[10] Al-Junaid taught that the forms that religion takes depend upon different cultural factors when he said that the colour that water seems to have is that of its container – on which Ibn al-Arabi commented: 'If he were to understand truly what Al-Junaid said regarding the colour of the water being that of its container, he would allow to every believer his belief and would recognize God in every form and in every belief.'[11] And another great Sufi, Jalal ul-din Rumi in the thirteenth century, wrote:

> Purity and impurity, sloth and diligence in worship,
> These mean nothing to Me.
>   I am apart from all that.
> Ways of worship are not to be ranked as better
> or worse than one another.
>
> Hindus do Hindu things.
> The Dravidian Muslims in India do what they do.
> It's all praise, and it's all right.
>
> It's not me that's glorified in acts of worship.
> It's the worshippers! I don't hear the words
> they say. I look inside at the humility.[12]

There is indeed probably no better 'soundbite' for the pluralist point of view than Rumi's words about the religions of his time,

---

[10]R. A. Nicholson, ed., *Eastern Poetry and Prose*, Cambridge University Press 1922, p. 148.

[11]Ibn al-Arabi, *The Bezels of Wisdom*, 283.

[12]Quoted in Karen Armstrong, *A History of God*, London: Heinemann (Mandarin) 1993, p. 278.

'The lamps are different, but the Light is the same'.[13] And in the West Nicholas of Cusa, in the fifteenth century, spoke in his book on peace between faiths (*De Pacis Fidei*) of there being 'only one religion in the variety of rites'.[14] Again, going back to India, in the sixteenth century the great Mughal emperor Akbar treated the plurality of religions within his empire in much the same ecumenical spirit as Ashoka in the third century. On a parallel Western track the early Quaker, William Penn (founder of Pennsylvania), wrote that 'The humble, meek, merciful, just, pious and devout souls are everywhere of one religion; and when death has taken off the mask they will know one another, though the divers liveries they wear here makes them strangers.'[15] So it is emphatically not the case that the religious pluralist vision is a product of modern Western culture. What *is* true, however, is that many of us in the West today, though not only in the West, are trying to develop this ancient insight under the impetus of our distinctively modern global awareness and with the tools of contemporary epistemological and religious studies.

## The post-modernist critique

**Phil:**     OK, so the pluralistic idea has ancient roots. But now for the political criticism. This comes in the post-modernist garb of those who see religious pluralism as an 'ideology' with an underlying 'political cosmology'[16] such that, it 'shamelessly reinforces the reification and privatization of life in advanced capitalist society'.[17] The charge is that religious pluralism is part

---

[13]*Rumi: Poet and Mystic*, trans. R. A. Nicholson, London and Boston: Unwin's Mandala Books 1978, p. 166.

[14]*Nicholas of Cusa on Interreligious Harmony*, trans. James E. Biechler and Lawrence Bond, Lewiston, NY: The Edwin Mellon Press 1990, p. 7.

[15]William Penn, *Some Fruits of Solitude* (1718), London: Constable 1926, pp. 99–100.

[16]Kenneth Surin, 'Towards a "Materialist" Critique of "Religious Pluralism": A Polemical Examination of the Discourse of John Hick and Wilfred Cantwell Smith', *The Thomist*, Vol. 53, no. 4 October 1989, p. 667. The article is reprinted in Ian Hamnett, (ed.), *Religious Pluralism and Unbelief*, op. cit.

[17]Kenneth Surin, ibid., p. 669.

of a new form of Western cultural imperialism which promotes what another writer calls the 'ambiguous imperial-humanist myth of our shared human attributes'.[18] It is, one writer suggests, 'no *mere* coincidence that "global" theologies have appeared at the precise historical moment when capitalism has entered its multinational stage'.[19] Indeed he believes that religious pluralism exists in 'a complex complicity' with 'global capitalist ideology'.[20]

**John:**    Yes, I'm familiar with this 'post-modernist' attack – though personally I'm not keen on the term 'post-modern' because it means such different things to different people. In fact, such is its range of meanings that I have myself been criticized by an evangelical writer for being a post-modernist [21] – which is perhaps even worse than being attacked *by* the post-modernists!

**Phil:**    Nevertheless the criticism I'm talking about does point to something real. It points to what many describe as the 'Americanization' of the world, seeing the USA as the main bearer today of a way of life which is rapidly encircling the globe, carried by radio and TV and manifested in an increasingly universal culture expressed in popular music, dress, the ubiquitous soap-operas, and so on. But behind this lies the exploiting power of the multinational corporations, international agencies, and the world-encompassing media, with McDonald's hamburger as the symbol of this new global culture. Intentionally or unintentionally it is undermining and destroying traditional ways of life, flattening them out into a kind of cultural pancake produced and

---

[18]Surin, ibid., p. 93, n. 2, quoting S.H. Mohanty, 'Us and Them: On the Philosophical Bases of Political Criticism', *The Yale Journal of Criticism*, Vol. 2 (1989), p. 13. See also John Milbank, 'The End of Dialogue' in Gavin D'Costa (ed.), *Christian Uniqueness Reconsidered*, Maryknoll, New York: Orbis 1990.

[19]Surin, ibid., pp. 665–6.

[20]Kenneth Surin, 'A Certain "Politics of Speech": "Religious Pluralism" in the Age of the McDonald's Hamburger', *Modern Theology*, Vol. 7, no. 1 (October 1990), p. 95, n.15. The article is reprinted, in a variant form that omits this particular sentence, in Gavin D'Costa, (ed.), *Christian Uniqueness Reconsidered*, op. cit.

[21]Robert Cook, 'Postmodernism, pluralism and John Hick', *Themelios*, Vol. 19, no. 1 (October 1993).

controlled by the great multinational corporations. And these critics claim that the world ecumenism supported by your colleagues and you is an aspect of this assault upon the differences of human culture, upon its concrete particularities, upon local traditions, by obliterating the differences between the religions. What do you say to this?

**John:** Well, it's a guilt by association argument, isn't it? Religious pluralism, with its global outlook, has become prominent at the time when the multinationals rule much of the world for their own profit by promoting a universal 'hamburger culture'; religious pluralism also has a global range; and so to condemn the evils of the multinationals' influence is at the same time to condemn religious pluralism! This seems to be the train of thought. But is it either logical or fair? Contemporary religious pluralism is part of the same world as multinational capitalism; but surely it doesn't follow that religious pluralism is an ally of international capitalism and its repressive universalizing effects.

**Phil:** So the ideology of a unitary world economy dominated by international capitalism, and the idea of the different world religions as responses to one ultimate divine reality, have nothing in common?

**John:** Well no, they do have in common our contemporary global awareness. And it's also true that all of us in North America and Europe share a general responsibility for the unjust and dangerous division of the world into a rich first world minority and a poor, and often desperately poor, third or two thirds world majority. But this general Western complicity in the economic injustice of our world applies impartially to religious exclusivists, inclusivists, and pluralists and also to post-modernists and everyone else in our societies, even including those who are personally working for world peace or against racism and against the unjust north–south economic divide. A Western post- modernist and a Western religious pluralist may be equally conscious of the evils of the international hegemony of the financial institutions, and yet be equally a part of the world that it has produced. But to use this as an argument specifically against religious pluralism is, surely, simply unfair and logically untenable.

## *Pluralism as homogenization*

**Phil:**   Put like that, it seems so. But perhaps the central charge is
that religious pluralism ignores or dismisses the concrete differences between the traditions, homogenizing them into a false
unity. A major theme of some of the post-modern writers is their
attack upon all 'totalizing' thinking that would force the complex
and variegated world into a single conceptual scheme. Such
thinking writes a global meta-narrative that subordinates all
individual and communal narratives, thus undermining 'alterity'
and eliminating the otherness of the Other. And critics apply this
to religious pluralism, which they say 'totalizes' the religious
realm, suppressing the mutual othernesses of the religions.
Religious pluralism, says one writer, 'is a comprehensive and
homogenizing historical scheme which assimilates to itself, and
thereby tames and domesticates, the practices and beliefs of the
different religious traditions'.[22] Again, he says, religious pluralism serves 'effectively to decompose or obscure that radical
historical particularity which is constitutive of the truly "other".
Where a certain Christian barbarism presumes its "superiority"
in order to justify the elimination or the conquest of the non-
Christian "other", this monological "pluralism" sedately but
ruthlessly domesticates and assimilates the "other" – *any* "other"
– in the name of a "world ecumenism".[23]

So the basic charge is that religious pluralism gives an
importantly different account of the great world religions from
that which each gives of itself. For in seeing the great traditions as
different responses to the same ultimate reality it dismisses their
differences as due to human factors built into the different
cultures of the earth. Isn't this to subordinate them to an over-all
theory that denies the concrete character of each and sees its
distinctive teachings as human symbols and myths?

Indeed, even more fundamentally, doesn't religious pluralism
assume that the religions are all trying to answer the same
question, whereas in fact they are each asking their own different

---

[22]Kenneth Surin, 'Towards a "Materialist" Critique', p. 666.
[23]Kenneth Surin, 'A Certain "Politics of Speech"', p. 77.

question? 'For instance, the central Jewish question, How can we keep life holy? seems to take quite a different aim than does the comparably central Theravada Buddhist question, How can I untie the knot of suffering?'.[24]

**John:**   Yes, its true that the religions ask different questions. But I want to suggest that these questions, whilst *specifically* different, are *generically* the same. They all presuppose a profound present lack, and the possibility of a radically better future; and they are all answers to the question, how to get from one to the other. In traditional Christian language they are all ways of asking, What must I do to be saved?

**Phil:**   But still you do seem to be fitting them all into a common pattern, which is provided by your own theory rather than arising out of what they each actually say.

## Leaving the religions as they are?

**John:**   I agree that there is a genuine issue here. But let me make a general point first, to set aside a misconception. The idea that each of the great world religions is a response to the ultimately real, and that each is a context of human salvation, does not mean that they are all the same, or that they all say the same thing,[25] or follow the same spiritual practices, or have identical moral codes and cultural life-styles. On the contrary, religious pluralism sees them as different, often very different, totalities consisting of distinctive ways of conceiving and experiencing the Real. And the practical outcome is not that there should be a new global religion, the same for everyone, but that the adherents of each of the existing world faiths should respond as fully as possible to the Real, the Ultimate, in their own way by devoutly living out their own tradition. So in this respect religious pluralism leaves the

---

[24]Steven G. Smith, 'Bowl climbing: The logic of religious question rivalry', *International Journal for Philosophy of Religion*, Vol. 36, no. 1 (August, 1994), p. 27.

[25]As is said, e.g., by Alister McGrath in 'A Particularist Approach' in Dennis Ockham and Timothy Phillips (eds), *More Than One Way?*, Grand Rapids, Michigan: Zondervan 1995.

different traditions just as they are. They are recognized, respected, affirmed as authentic contexts of salvation/liberation, each with its own unique character and historical particularities.

**Phil:** But not, it would seem, their own beliefs. For you deny, don't you, some of the essential doctrines of each – for example, the Christian claim that Jesus was God incarnate, and the claims of Buddhist and Hindu mystics to a direct unmediated experience of ultimate reality, unaffected by the ideas of their own tradition? You say that the former is a metaphor for Jesus' significance to Christians, as the one who has made God real to us; and that the latter has to be qualified by the fact that the mystics of different traditions produce different and incompatible reports of the ultimate. But in that case it seems that, as one critic says, 'Hick can accommodate troublesome doctrines by reinterpreting them so as to eliminate problematic elements; but the price of such reinterpretation is that the reinterpreted doctrines bear little resemblance to the doctrines held in the respective traditions'.[26] Right?

**John:** Yes and no. On the one hand religious pluralism leaves the different doctrinal systems intact within their own religious traditions, but on the other hand it proposes the meta-theory that these traditions, as complex totalities, are different human responses to the Real.[27]

**Phil:** But within your meta-theory, the pluralistic hypothesis, the different doctrinal systems are downgraded from conflicting universal and absolute truth-claims to local truths valid only within a given tradition.

**John:** Yes, that's so in the case of their conflicting particularities. But let's remember the basic problem we're trying to solve. Not more than one of these rival belief-systems could be finally and universally true, and yet the traditions within which they

---

[26]Harold Netland, 'Professor Hick on Religious Pluralism', *Religious Studies*, Vol. 22, no. 2 (June 1986), p. 256. See also his *Dissonant Voices: Religious Pluralism and the Question of Truth*, Grand Rapids, Michigan: Eerdmans and Leicester, England: Apollos 1991, pp. 221–33.

[27]This point is well made by Sumner B. Twiss, 'The Philosophy of Religious Pluralism: A Critical Appraisal of Hick and His Critics', *The Journal of Religion*, Vol. 70, no. 4 (October 1990).

function seem, when judged by their fruits, to be more or less equally valid responses to the Real. Now the distinction between the Real in itself and the Real as variously humanly thought and experienced enables us to understand how this can be: namely, the differing belief-systems are beliefs about *different* manifestations of the Real. They're not mutually conflicting beliefs, because they're beliefs about different phenomenal realities. It's in this sense that they are reduced or 'downgraded' in their scope.

**Phil:** And that's a pretty radical reinterpretation, isn't it?

**John:** Yes; but we really do have to make a choice between a one-tradition absolutism and a genuinely pluralistic interpretation of the global religious situation.

**Phil:** I suspect that faced with this choice most believers within the different traditions will opt for the absolute truth of their own tradition. But returning to the idea of leaving the different belief-systems intact within their respective traditions, don't you nevertheless in your capacity as a Christian theologian want to revise our traditional system of doctrine?

**John:** Yes, and you're right to imply a distinction between the work of a theologian, which is internal to a particular tradition, and that of a philosopher of religion. Although the philosophy of religion in the West has until fairly recently meant in practice the philosophy of the Christian religion, or more broadly of the Judaeo-Christian tradition, it's subject matter is properly religion in all its variety of forms around the world and throughout history. Of course in fact the modern explosion of knowledge is too great for any one person to master it all, and most philosophers of religion who recognize the global scope of their subject have to be content to take account of what are usually called the 'great world faiths'.

**Phil:** So as a philosopher of religion on Mondays, Tuesdays and Wednesdays you propose the pluralistic hypothesis, and as a Christian theologian on Thursdays, Fridays, Saturdays, and presumably particularly on Sundays, you do what?

**John:** On those days, as a theologian who has – earlier in the week – accepted the pluralistic hypothesis, I try to contribute to the on-going development of Christian thought in the light of our knowledge of the wider religious world. After all, right from the beginning the Christian belief-system has been changing all the time, sometimes slowly and sometimes rapidly, in response to developments in human knowledge and experience. Occasionally a major change, a 'paradigm shift', occurs, as for example in the nineteenth-century response to evolution theory and the critical study of the Bible. And I believe that an equally major shift is needed today in response to our new awareness of the other world religions.

**Phil:**   Well that will be something for Grace to take up with you later. But apart from their belief-systems you think that the religions are all right as they are. No critical discriminations needed?[28]

**John:**   Well, no, I'm afraid we can't say that. First of all, not by any means every religious movement – in the broad family-resemblance sense of 'religious' – is salvific: not Nazism, or Satanism, or the Jim Jones or the Waco phenomena, for example. And secondly, that the great world religions *are* contexts of salvation/liberation doesn't mean that they are perfect contexts, or that every aspect of them is equally salvific or indeed salvific at all. There are elements within each that have little or no religious value, or indeed that work directly against the salvific trans-formation. Each one of the world religions has been responsible for great evils as well as great goods. Their exclusive absolutisms have created communal conflicts and have been used both to validate war and to intensify its savagery. Has not each side in virtually every war invoked the name of God? Again, some religious beliefs have led to harmful practices, including human sacrifice, the repression of women, the slaughter of Jews, the torture of witches, opposition to planned parenthood, dis-crimination against homosexuals. Dogmatism has led to thought-control and the persecution of intellectual deviants and innovators. Exploitation and slavery have been given religious justification. And so that a religion is as a totality in some

---

[28]E.g., 'The pluralistic approach represented in *The Myth of Christian Uniqueness* seems in general to advocate accepting all religions on their own terms without discriminating between the spirits within them', M. M. Thomas in *Christian Uniqueness Reconsidered*, op. cit., p. 57. 'Hick's

important degree a context of salvation/liberation doesn't mean that there is no scope for discrimination, criticism, and sometimes outright condemnation. But such criticism, whether of our own tradition or of another, should always be specific, directed to particular events, individuals, and situations, and should aim at their correction.

## Pluralism contradicts each religion's own self-understanding

**Phil:**   OK, and we must come later to the question of the criteria. But to stay for the moment with our original question, is there not a clear sense in which religious pluralism *does* give a different status to the various traditions and their teachings from that which they give themselves? To put the point strongly, in the words of a critic, 'It is curious that those wishing better relationships between religions and who are anxious to dispose of exclusivist claims, end up inadvertently not respecting the integrity of the different traditions and the seriousness and absoluteness of their claims and thereby erect a new exclusivism'.[29]

**John:**   Yes, I have to agree that there's a sense in which religious pluralism does, as you say, give a different status to the various traditions and their teachings from that which they give themselves. But I want to claim that in the sense in which this is so, it is a virtue and not a vice.

**Phil:**   How so? Let's take first conceptions of the ultimately real – as the Holy Trinity of Christianity, or as the Allah of Islam, or as the Brahman of the Indian religions, and so on. You've been taken to mean that, for example, the Christian term 'God' and the Buddhist term 'Emptiness' (*sunyata*), and the Hindu term

---

refusal to take an evaluative position in relation to other religions', Alister McGrath, 'The Challenge of Pluralism for the Contemporary Christian Church' in *The Challenge of Religious Pluralism*, Wheaton, Illinois: Wheaton College 1992, p. 240.

[29] Gavin D'Costa, 'Whose Objectivity? Which Neutrality? The Doomed Quest for a Neutral Vantage Point from which to Judge Religions', *Religious Studies*, Vol. 29, no. 1 (March 1993), p. 94.

'Brahman', and so on, are all different names for the same referent. Is that correct?

**John:**   No, not at all. As I said just now, in my view each refers to a different persona or impersona of the Real. These different foci of worship and meditation are not identical with the Real in itself, but are the Real as humanly pictured in different ways. Using the Kantian analogy, they are phenomenal manifestations of the noumenal Real-in-itself.

**Phil:**   And you say that each is partly a human projection, as a joint product of the universal presence of the Real and of a particular human conceptual scheme and its associated spiritual practices?

**John:**   Yes, just so.

**Phil:**   And incidentally, as a slight digression at this point, some have complained that you are using Kant in a rather cavalier fashion, and that his philosophy is much more complex than one would think from what you say.[30]

**John:**   Well yes, of course. I am only using here one aspect of his vast *corpus*, and applying it to the epistemology of religion. Nor do I suggest that Kant himself would have approved of this. He had a different religious epistemology, according to which God is a necessary postulate of practical reason. But it was Kant above all who made it clear that the human mind is always active in perception and always plays a creative role in our awareness of our physical environment. I am suggesting that this is also true in relation to our ultimate divine environment. But there is the important difference that whereas Kant spoke of our experiencing in terms of concepts (such as thinghood and causality) which are universal because innate to the human mind, our religious concepts (such as deity, trinity, the absolute, emptiness) vary from culture to culture.

**Phil:**   Yes. And of course there are also critics who are aware that you are taking a basic thought from Kant rather than his entire system, but who nevertheless regard Kant, together with

---

[30]E.g., Paul Eddy, 'Religious Pluralism and the Divine: Another Look at John Hick's Neo-Kantian Proposal', *Religious Studies*, Vol. 30, no. 4 (December 1994), pp. 473–8.

his basic thought, as the great misleader of modern philosophy.[31]

**John:** I know; and I simply disagree with them about this. I regard Kant as, on the whole, the most penetrating and illuminating, as well as the most influential, of modern Western philosophers.

**Phil:** Well, be that as it may, let's come back to my point that your use of Kant leads you to see the world religions differently from the way in which each sees itself. Because none of them sees itself, does it, as constituting one way amongst others of perceiving the divine?

**John:** No, I must agree that in their central traditional forms they don't. This is because what each religion says about the Ultimate, the Real, has been developed within its own conceptual world. And so for Christianity the Ultimate just is the Holy Trinity; for Islam it just is the strictly unitary Allah; for Hinduism, it just is the infinite consciousness of Brahman; and so on. This would be unproblematic if all human beings had the same religion – whichever that might be. The problem arises when you take account of the plurality of claimed awarenesses of the Real within the different world faiths. And once you've concluded that their moral and spiritual fruits seem to be, although different, more or less equally valuable, you are driven to the realization that the Real is capable of being humanly thought and experienced in more than one way. This is of course precisely what religious pluralism proposes, and its justification is simply that this is a more realistic view because it takes account of a wider range of data than any one of the traditional absolutisms.

**Phil:** But still this more realistic view, as you call it, does depart from what each tradition says about itself.

**John:** Yes, it does and it must. This has to be recognized by anyone who is trying to develop an understanding of religious

---

[31]E.g. Brian Hebblethwaite, 'John Hick and the Question of Truth in Religion' in Arvind Sharma, (ed.), *God, Truth and Reality: Essays in Honour of John Hick*, London: Macmillan, and New York: St Martin's Press 1993, pp. 132–3

diversity.[32] Indeed, isn't it evident that any account of the human religious situation which fully acknowledges the religious value of the great world traditions must differ from the account traditionally given by any one of them?

**Phil:**   Why?

**John:**   Because each, left to itself, affirms its own uniquely full salvific access to the Real, and this affirmation has developed into a structure of belief which can only accommodate other traditions by subordinating them to itself, whether as total errors or as partial truths. And so a global interpretation which starts from the rough salvific parity of the great traditions will not be identical with the belief-system of any one of them. This is why we have either to seek a more comprehensive view, or else each return to the absolutism of our own tradition, with Christians, Jews, Muslims, Hindus, Buddhists and so on each affirming the unique superiority of their own path.

**Phil:**   So you're not really bothered by the fact that the pluralistic account of the situation actually contradicts the account given by each one of the historical religions? Doesn't that sound rather presumptuous?

**John:**   In a way no doubt it does. But you have to face up to the fact that no hypothesis about the relation between the different world religions – unless it simply affirms the truth of one and the falsity of the rest – is going to be congruent with the belief-system of one of them to the exclusion of the others. To complain about this is simply to turn one's back on the whole project of a religious interpretation of religion in its wide variety of forms. One cannot seek such a comprehensive interpretation and then disqualify any proposal that doesn't simply replicate the particular doctrines of one's own tradition. The options are either to affirm the absolute truth of one's own tradition, or go for some form of pluralistic

---

[32]So, e.g., Keith Ward says of his own suggestion about the development of the different traditions through their mutual interactions and their ever-wider integration of other knowledge, 'I am aware, of course, that perhaps the majority of major religious faiths would not accept the way I have put things in this chapter – especially in regard to the necessity fully to assimilate post-critical attitudes', in *Religious Pluralism and Unbelief*, op. cit., pp. 25–6.

view – or of course have no view and simply regard the whole matter as a mystery.

**Phil:** I think I'd better leave it to our listeners to make their own judgment about that. But let's look at another criticism.

## The pluralist's claim to a privileged vantage point

This is that the religious pluralist claims a privileged vantage point from which to see the different religions and the relations between them in a way which is hidden from the religions themselves. One critic has called this 'the myth of the neutral observer'[33] – and another, more grandiosely, 'a timeless logos enjoying time-transcending encounters with an unchanging reality'.[34] Thus in the ancient Indian parable of the elephant and the blind men,[35] one feeling a leg and reporting that the elephant is a tree, another feeling the trunk and reporting that it is a huge snake, another feeling the tail and reporting that the elephant is a rope, and so on, the teller of the parable is assumed not be to blind but to be able to view the entire scene. In the case of the religious pluralism this is, in the words of one writer, 'the immensely arrogant claim of one who sees the full truth, which all the world's religions are only groping after'.[36] Isn't religious pluralism arrogant in this way?

**John:** Well, it certainly would be if it made such a claim. But the

---

[33]Eric O. Springsted, 'Conditions of Dialogue: John Hick and Simone Weil', *Journal of Religion*, Vol. 72, no. 1 (January 1992), pp. 22f.

[34]John Milbank in *Christian Uniqueness Reconsidered*, op. cit., p. 174.

[35]Gavin D'Costa, in 'Elephants, Ropes and a Christian Theology of Religions' (*Theology*, Vol. 88, no. 724, July 1985) refers to me as 'a leading blind-men-elephant spokesman' (p. 260) on the basis of a single reference to the parable (*God and the Universe of Faiths*, op. cit., p. 140), where I point out its limitations, having introduced it as an example of a pervasive Indian way of thinking. On this slender basis D'Costa speaks of the book as a whole my 'book propounding the blind-men-elephant thesis' (p. 265). Peter Byrne ('John Hick's Philosophy of World Religions', *Scottish Journal of Theology*, Vol. 35, no. 4, August 1982), and Philip Almond ('John Hick's Copernican Theology', *Theology*, Vol. 86, no. 709, January 1983), and Michael Barnes (*Religions in Conversation*, London: SPCK 1989, p. 78) each in their own way indulge in this exaggeration.

[36]Lesslie Newbigin, *The Gospel in a Pluralist Society*, op. cit., p. 10.

pluralistic hypothesis is arrived at inductively, from ground level. I start out as one committed to the faith that Christian religious experience is not purely a projection but is at the same time a cognitive response to a transcendent reality; and its fruits in Christian lives confirm this to me. I then notice that there are other great world religions likewise reporting their own different forms of religious experience, the cognitive character of which is supported in the same way. And so I have to extend to them the principle that religious experience constitutes a valid basis for religious belief. But I now have on my hands the problem of several conflicting sets of truth-claims which are equally well based in religious experience and confirmed by their fruits. In order to understand this situation I form the hypothesis of an ultimate divine reality which is being differently conceived, and therefore differently experienced, from within the different religio-cultural ways of being human. This is an hypothesis offered to explain, from a religious as distinguished from a naturalistic point of view, the facts described by the historians of religion.[37] It is an explanatory theory; and I suggest that critics who don't like it should occupy themselves in trying to produce a better one.

**Phil:**   That the pluralistic hypothesis is, you say, an hypothesis connects with Keith Ward's discussion of it in his recent *Religion and Revelation*, where he sets out what he thinks is your argument in six successive propositions and then shows that these do not form a logically sound argument.[38] Is he right in assuming

---

[37]Joseph Runzo, in 'God, Commitment, and Other Faiths: Pluralism Vs Relativism' (*Faith and Philosophy*, Vol. 5, no. 4, October 1988) makes it a point of criticism that religious pluralism 'would amount to a hypothesis or theory about the world religions', p. 258. But it is explicitly this (as are his own and other alternative proposals, whether or not acknowledged as such), and I cannot see that it is a valid criticism of an hypothesis that it is an hypothesis! Owen Thomas ('Religious Plurality and Contemporary Philo-sophy: A Critical Survey', *Harvard Theological Review*, Vol. 82, no. 2, 1994) makes it a point of criticism that 'every pluralist universal theory or overarching framework is always the elaboration of a particular perspective' (p. 207). Of course it is; and so is every other theory about anything! Thomas adds in the same sentence the perplexing *non-sequitur* 'and thus has the form of an inclusivism'.

[38]Keith Ward, *Religion and Revelation*, op. cit., pp. 313–16.

that you are trying to offer a logically irresistible argument for your hypothesis? Or has he misunderstood you?

**John:** The latter. As I've always insisted, the hypothesis is offered as the 'best explanation', i.e. the most comprehensive and economical explanation, from a religious point of view, of the facts of the history of religions. A proffered 'best explanation' is not a proof, because it is always open to someone else to come forward and offer what they believe is a better explanation. And so the right response of someone who does not like my proposed explanation is not to complain that it is not proved but to work out a viable alternative.

## Truth-claims and myths

**Phil:** Oh, I'm not advocating any position myself but simply relaying others' criticisms of the pluralistic hypothesis. So let me put again the charge that it involves a downgrading of the doctrines of the different religions from the status of absolute truths to that of relative, mythic, metaphorical, or symbolic truths. For you say this, don't you, concerning some of the most central affirmations of each of the great traditions?

**John:** Yes. I want to say that what is literally or analogically true of, say, the heavenly Parent of Christian belief – for example, that God is loving, like an ideal parent – is mythologically true of the Real in itself.

**Phil:** And what do you mean by 'mythologically true'?

**John:** I mean by a myth a story that is not literally true but that has the power to evoke in its hearers a practical response to the myth's referent – a true myth being of course one that evokes an *appropriate* response. The truthfulness of a myth is thus a practical truthfulness, consisting in its capacity to orient us rightly in our lives. In so far as the heavenly Parent is an authentic manifestation of the Real, to think of the Real as an ideal parent is to think in a way that can orient us rightly to the Real, evoking in us a trust which can pervade our lives and free us to love our neighbour. And of course I want to give a parallel account of the language about the Ultimate used by each of the other world religions.

**Phil:**   I suppose this has some affinity with Tillich's doctrine of the symbolic character of religious language. But are there not other levels of conflicting truth-claims?

## Conflicting metaphysical beliefs

**John:**   Yes, another consists of metaphysical beliefs which the different traditions have adopted, such as beliefs about the origin of the universe, as created *ex nihilo* or as emanated or beginninglessly in existence; about human destiny in heaven and hell immediately after death, or this plus purgatory, or in repeated reincarnations either of the conscious self or of a basic dispositional (karmic) structure in this or other worlds, or in an eventual transcending of individual selfhood, or a mixture of these;[39] and, again, beliefs about angels and demons and other spheres of existence, and so on.

**Phil:**   And what do you say about these matters?

**John:**   That we should be very cautious in making knowledge-claims in these areas. We don't really know at present, in any strict sense of 'know', whether the physical universe is beginningless or had an absolute beginning a finite number of years ago; whether after death we are born again into another finite life or emerge into an eternal heavenly state, and so on. Here I would commend the Buddha's teaching about the 'undetermined questions' (*avyakata*). The issues I've just mentioned were in fact among his examples. When asked about them he refused to answer, saying that these are things we do not need to know in order to attain liberation, or awakening, and that to make it our great business to find out would only distract us from the quest for liberation. This seems to me realistic – in spite of the fact that some of us are paid to spend our time working on these questions! I think we have to accept that our opinions in these areas are only opinions, and that it is not necessary for salvation that our present opinions turn out to be true.

---

[39]Some readers may be interested to pursue these possibilities in my *Death and Eternal Life*, 1976 (London: Macmillan 1985, and Louisville: Westminster/John Knox 1994).

**Phil:** You mean, it doesn't make any difference whether, for example, the universe began some fifteen billion years ago or has always existed?

**John:** No, it does of course make a difference in that these are two genuinely different and mutually exclusive possibilities. But it doesn't make any practical difference to us now in the living of our lives. We can live religiously with either cosmological scenario; and if one of them seems to some people to be obviously true and the other obviously false, this is because they were raised in one culture rather than another. Neither is in fact at present obviously true in any objective sense.

**Phil:** But what about the cultures that cherish these ideas? Hasn't the Christian belief in divine creation out of nothing, and thus in the universe having a definite and discoverable structure, made modern science possible? Wasn't it A. N. Whitehead who suggested that 'faith in the possibility of science, generated antecedently to the development of modern scientific theory, is an unconscious derivative from medieval theology'?[40] And hasn't the Indian belief in a cyclical universe, continually created and destroyed and re-created, been incompatible with scientific discovery?

**John:** No, I don't think so. It's certainly true that science presupposes an orderly universe, functioning according to regularities which can be observed, so that experiments can be devised and explanatory theories developed. But all the great world faiths see the world process as proceeding in an orderly and law-governed way; and both ancient Chinese and mediaeval Islamic science made some real progress. None of the world faiths sees the universe as a chaos that is unamenable to systematic observation and theorizing – although most of them, including Christianity, have also believed in miracles which arbitrarily disrupt the order of nature and are thus incompatible with the scientific project.

**Phil:** But it's true, surely, that the vast modern expansion of science began on Christian soil.

**John:** Yes, it is. But this can hardly be regarded as a natural

---

[40]A. N. Whitehead, *Science and the Modern World*, Cambridge University Press 1926, p. 18.

outcome of distinctively Christian ideas. For if it were, why did Christian civilization proceed for more than a thousand years without producing science? And why, when modern science did begin, did the church try to suppress it? The church was no friend to Copernicus or Galileo or Lyell or Darwin or Huxley. The intellectual stimulus behind modern Western science seems to have been the Renaissance rediscovery of the Greek spirit of free inquiry, and as the sciences rapidly became autonomous, and astronomy and later geology produced discoveries that conflicted with the traditional Christian world-view, the church reacted violently against them. Hence the great science versus religion debates of the nineteenth century.

**Phil:** So you don't put modern science down to the credit of Christianity?

**John:** No, modern science, with technology as its practical application, is an autonomous enterprise which, having begun in Europe, has rapidly spread around the globe; and there are today plenty of distinguished physicists and workers in other sciences whose background is Jewish, Hindu, Buddhist, Muslim as well as Christian.

And, if I may add one more point, the cyclical idea that we associate with Eastern thought has become one of the live options in scientific cosmology today in the model of a beginninglessly expanding and contracting universe. We will probably eventually be able to determine whether the amount of matter in the universe is or is not sufficient by its gravitational pull to reverse the present expansion, opening up the possibility of a beginningless and endless series of expansions and contractions, or whether on the contrary the big bang of some ten to fifteen billion years ago was an absolute beginning. But if it should turn out that the cyclical model is correct, this would not be a blow to a rational form of Christianity, any more than the discovery that the big bang was unique would be a blow to a rational form of Hindu or Buddhist belief. The central truths of religion do not depend upon such questions.

**Phil:** I'm not sure whether I can agree with that or not. But, either way, let's move now to the remaining kind of conflicting truth-claims, historical ones.

## Conflicting historical truth-claims

**John:** Yes. There aren't in fact many such conflicts between the religions because, generally speaking, each tradition cherishes its own separate strand of remembered history. But there are a few instances within the biblical history that is common to Judaism, Christianity and Islam.

**Phil:** For instance?

**John:** For instance, there is the disagreement between Judaism and Islam about Isaac and Ishmael, traditionally regarded as forefathers of the Jewish and Arab peoples respectively. According to the Torah (Genesis, chapter 22) Abraham nearly sacrificed his son Isaac. According to the Qur'an (Surah 37, 100–108) Abraham dreamed of sacrificing a son, who is not named in the text but whom Muslim tradition takes to be Ishmael. In each story the son figures in a test, as a result of which Abraham and his progency are divinely blessed. But the figure of Abraham belongs to pre-historical saga, and disputes about him cannot be settled by historical evidence. Their significance lies in the use of Isaac and Ishmael as symbols of Jewish and Arab pre-eminence. But when Jews and Muslims are no longer interested in claiming this kind of pre-eminence, but recognize (as indeed many do) that God is equally worshipped within both traditions, the Abraham story will cease to be a matter of contention between them.

**Phil:** And the other instance?

**John:** This is the Christian belief that Jesus died on the cross versus the Muslim belief that he only appeared to die. In this case there is extra-biblical evidence, in the near-contemporary references in Josephus and Tacitus, to Jesus' execution under Pontius Pilate. There is, however, the complication that the Qur'an (4. 157) says that this *appeared* to be the case; so that the historical evidence might be the same on the Qur'anic account! One importance of the difference lies of course in the centrality of Jesus' death to the various Christian atonement doctrines.[41] So there is a significant issue here. But apart from these two instances

---

[41]For a critique of these, see my *The Metaphor of God Incarnate*, op. cit., chs 11–12.

I cannot at the moment think of any other conflicting historical beliefs between the religions – though there may be others of which I'm not aware. All that I can say about any such disputes is that they can only properly be settled, if indeed they can be settled at all, by historical evidence.

# 3

# The Real, Ineffability, and Criteria

## *The ineffability of the Real*

**Phil:** All right. I'll turn now to a different criticism, and a very fundamental one, offered by several writers. This concerns the Real as ineffable – as lying beyond the range of our human conceptual systems. That's right isn't it?

**John:** Yes.

**Phil:** You've supported this by claiming that the idea of the ineffability, or in Eastern terms the formlessness, of the Ultimate is taught within all the great traditions. How do you substantiate that?

**John:** I could give innumerable quotations, but here are a few representative ones. Within Hinduism, the Upanishads say of Brahman, 'There the eye goes not, speech goes not, nor the mind',[1] and that Brahman is that 'before which words recoil, and to which no understanding has ever attained'.[2] Or again, 'Thou art formless: thy only form is our knowledge of thee'.[3] From Sikhism, 'By thinking I cannot obtain a conception of Him, even though I think hundreds of thousands of times'.[4] The *Tao Te*

---

[1] *Mundaka* Upanishad, 1. 3, trans. Radhakrishnan, *The Principal Upanishads*, London: Allen & Unwin and New York: Humanities Press 1969, p. 688.

[2] *Taittiriya* Upanishad, II. 4. 1, trans. Radhakrishnan, op. cit., p. 552.

[3] *Yogava'sistha*, I, 28. V. L. Parrisikar (ed.), *Srimad – Valmiki – Maharsi – Pannitah Yogava'sistha*, I, 2nd ed., Bombay: Tukaram Javaji 1978, p. 144.

[4] Guru Nanak's *Japji*, Ninian Smart and Richard Hecht (eds), *Sacred Texts of the World*, London: Macmillan 1982, and New York: Crossroad p. 330.

*Ching* declares that 'The Tao that can be expressed is not the eternal Tao'.[5] Within Buddhism ultimate reality is referred to, within the Mahayana tradition, as *sunyata*, emptiness. As D. T. Suzuki explains, 'To say that reality is "empty" means that it goes beyond definability, and cannot be qualified as this or that'.[6] In other words, it is empty of everything that the human mind projects in its activity of awareness. Again, in another formulation the ultimate is referred to as the Dharmakaya, the ineffable Truth-body of the universal Buddha-nature, which becomes concrete and nameable in the heavenly Buddhas of the Sambhogakaya and in the incarnate historical Buddhas of the Nirmanakaya. Within the mystical strands of Judaism and Islam, *En Sof*, the Infinite, and *al-Haqq*, the Real, are beyond all human thought forms. And within Christianity, in the early period Gregory of Nyssa wrote that God is 'incapable of being grasped by any term, or any idea, or any other device of our apprehension, remaining beyond the reach not only of the human but of the angelic and all supramundane intelligence, unthinkable, unutterable, above all expression in words'.[7] Later, St Thomas Aquinas wrote that 'by its immensity the divine substance surpasses every form that our intellect reaches',[8] and that 'what God is transcends all that we understand of him'.[9] Indeed, I think we can say that all serious religious thought affirms that the Ultimate, in its infinite divine reality, is utterly beyond our comprehension.

**Phil:**   And yet on the other hand, certainly so far as Christianity

---

[5]*Tao Te Ching*, I, trans. Ch'u Ta-Kao, London and Boston: Mandala Books 1982.

[6]D. T. Suzuki, 'The Buddhist Conception of Reality' in Frederick Franck, (ed.), *The Buddha Eye*, New York: Crossroad 1982, p. 103.

[7]Gregory of Nyssa, *Against Eunomius*, I, 42, Philip Schaff and Henry Wace, (eds), *Nicene and Post-Nicene Fathers*, Series 2, Vol. V, Grand Rapids, Michigan: Eerdmans 1956, p. 99.

[8]St Thomas, *In librum De Causis*, 6. Quoted by F. C. Coplestone, *Aquinas*, Harmondsworth: Penguin Books 1955, pp. 131–2.

[9]St Thomas, *De Potentia*, Q. 7, art. 5, quoted by Hans Küng, *Great Christian Thinkers*, London: SCM Press and New York: Continuum 1994, p. 126.

is concerned, thinkers have always also insisted upon the positive divine attributes.[10]

**John:**  Yes, that's right. Christian theology has always wanted both to acknowledge the ultimate ineffability of the divine nature, and yet at the same time, for devotional and liturgical purposes, to speak of God as a personal presence with distinctive human-like qualities. But the relation between these seeming incompatibles has never been made clear. I am suggesting, however, that it can be made clear by distinguishing between God in God's infinite self-existent being, beyond our conceptual grasp, and God as known to us in humanly conceivable and experienceable ways.

**Phil:**  So according to you, God *a se* – or the Real *an sich* – cannot be spoken about in human terms?

**John:**  Yes that's right, with one minor qualification. This is that logic alone can generate purely formal statements about anything, including the ineffable. For to say that the Real cannot be spoken about in human language is already to have said something about it in human language – namely that it cannot be spoken about in human language! But this is a logical triviality with no significant consequences. We should note it, and then pass on.

**Phil:**  But is it really so trivial? One writer has pointed out that 'if X has the property of being able to be referred to, this reference must be accomplished by ostentation [i.e. pointing or otherwise showing] or description. Ostentation is ruled out by definition, for an object which transcends the universe. So any reference must be made by description; X must be identified as "the X which . . ."'.[11] Isn't that right?

**John:**  Yes, in that it would not make sense to speak of an X about which nothing can be said except that it can be referred

---

[10]Cf. Paul Eddy, 'Religious Pluralism and the Divine', *Religious Studies*, Vol. 30, no. 3 (December 1994), pp. 469–73.

[11]Keith Ward, 'Truth and the Diversity of Religions', *Religious Studies*, Vol. 26, no. 1 (March 1990), p. 9. See also Keith Yandell, 'Some Varieties of Religious Pluralism' in J. Kellenberger (ed.), *Inter-Religious Models and Criteria*, London: Macmillan and New York: St Martin's Press 1993, pp. 195–8.

to. But that's not the case here. This X is postulated as that which there must be if religious experience, in its diversity of forms, is not purely imaginative projection but is also a response to a transcendent reality.[12]

**Phil:** Or, presumably, realities.

**John:** I don't think so; but can we take that question separately later?

**Phil:** OK. So at the moment we are left with the view that the Real has no humanly conceivable qualities (other than the purely formal ones you've just mentioned) and therefore cannot be said to be in itself personal or impersonal, one or many, good or evil, just or unjust, substance or process, active or passive, purposive or non-purposive. So it seems that it would be a misunderstanding to think of the Real as a 'thing' or substance of some kind, as some have assumed you to mean.[13]

**John:** Yes it would.

**Phil:** But if the Real is not a thing of any kind then, surely, it is nothing.

**John:** No. It is no *thing*, but not nothing!

**Phil:** Explain.

**John:** It is not a *thing* because it trancends all our thing-concepts, including our religious thing-concepts. But on the other hand it is not nothing: it is that reality in virtue of which, through our response to one or other of its manifestations as the God figures or the non-personal Absolutes, we can arrive at the blessed unselfcentred state which is our highest good.

**Phil:** So is this ultimate reality which is no thing, and yet not nothing, the same as *sunyata* – the Emptyness or Void – of which Buddhists in the Mahayana tradition speak?

**John:** That depends on how you interpret *sunyata* – about which there is a whole literature. If you understand the idea of

---

[12]I should like to add here that Keith Ward (in ibid., p. 10), followed by Paul Eddy ('Religious Pluralism and the Divine', op. cit., p. 472), are right in pointing out that Anselm's concept of God as 'that than which no greater can be conceived' is not a good example, as I had once suggested, of a purely formal concept; and I accept their correction.

[13]E.g. Ninian Smart in 'A Contemplation of Absolutes' in *God, Truth and Reality*, op. cit.

*sunyata* as indicating that the ultimately real is completely and utterly empty of everything that the human mind projects in its activity of cognition, then this does indeed apply to what I mean by the Real. It – in English one has to say either 'he', 'she' or 'it', and 'it' is the least misleading – has no humanly conceivable qualities.

**Phil:** So it is not, for example, personal?

**John:** No. But in denying that the Real is personal one is not saying that it is impersonal, but rather that the personal-impersonal dualism does not apply here. To ask whether the Real is personal or impersonal would be misleading, because it presupposes that it's an entity of the kind that *could* be personal or impersonal. And the same with the other dualisms.

**Phil:** All right. But I'd still like to press you further about ineffability. According to you, the statement that 'God is good, loving, purposeful' is literally true of the heavenly Parent of Jesus' teaching and mythologically true of the Real in itself. But could we not equally well, or perhaps better, say that it is *analogically* true of the Real in itself?[14] For if the heavenly Parent is an authentic manifestation, or appearance, or experiencable form of the Real, must not the heavenly Parent's attributes have their analogical counterparts in the Real itself? Even if the Real is not good or loving in the humanly understandable way in which the heavenly Parent is, yet surely there must be in the nature of the Real something *analogous* to goodness and love. For otherwise how could the heavenly Parent be a genuine manifestation of the Real? Why could not an unloving, evil deity be an authentic manifestation of the Real? Only, surely, because the Real has a nature that is reflected in goodness and love but not in evil and hatred. So the Real must have a nature that includes its own analogues of goodness and love.

**John:** I see the force of your argument. Nevertheless I don't think it can be accepted, because it violates the principle that

---

[14]This is well argued by Bernard J. Verkamp in 'Hick's Interpretation of Religious Pluralism', *International Journal for Philosophy of Religion*, Vol. 30, no. 2 (October 1991), pp. 111–12.

any comprehensive interpretation of religion must take account of all the major traditions, and not just of one's own.

**Phil:**   How do you mean?

**John:**   Well, let us suppose, as a thought experiment, that the Real has its analogues of the various attributes of the heavenly Parent, which will include personality, love, goodness, compassion, justice, mercy, power, intentions, consciousness, knowledge. We now have to add that the Real also has its analogues of the attributes of its other authentic personae and impersonae. But this quickly leads to manifest contradictions. The description of the Real will now have to include its being analogically personal and also its being analogically non-personal, analogically conscious and also analogically non-conscious, analogically purposive and also analogically non-purposive, analogous to a substance and also analogous to a non-substantial process, and so on. The more you add to the list the more incoherent it becomes. So rather than get into such a morass of impossibilities it seems to me that we should acknowledge that all these attributes are components of our human conceptual repertoire. But a comprehensive interpretation of religion requires us to postulate an ultimate reality which exceeds that conceptual repertoire, and is thus from our point of view ineffable or formless. It has its own nature, presumably infinite in richness, but that nature is not thinkable in our human terms – and indeed even the concept of a nature, or an essence, belongs to the network of human concepts which the Real totally transcends.

**Phil:**   But you said in your lecture, and I quote, 'we cannot describe [the Real] as it is in itself, but only as it is thought and experienced in human terms – from within some traditions as personal and from within others as nonpersonal, and from within all of them as being, in relation to human life, good or benign or gracious, as the ground of all human transformation from unhappy self-centredness to the blessedness that is variously thought and experienced as eternal life/peace with God/nirvana/moksha/satori' (above p. 28). But how can you describe the Real as good, benign, gracious, which are humanly conceivable attributes, and at the same time insist that it has no humanly conceivable attributes?

**John:**   Well, you see, I do not describe the Real *in itself* as good, or benign, or gracious. But in relation to us – that is, in terms of the difference that it makes to us – it is good as the ground of the transformed state which is our highest good. So the sense in which the Real is good, benign, gracious is analogous to that in which the sun is, from our point of view, good, friendly, life-giving. (Poets have spoken, for example, of 'the blessed sun himself' and how 'the sun shines sweetly on'.) The life-giving warmth of the sun is the ground, or the *sine qua non*, of our existence and our flourishing. Likewise, the Real is the necessary condition of our existence and our highest good. It is in this sense that we can speak of the Real as being, in relation to us, good, benign, gracious. But when we describe the Real in itself in these terms we are speaking mythologically rather than literally.

**Phil:**   It sounds, then, as though your position is much more radical than the kind of pluralism advocated by Keith Ward. He also affirms a form of religious pluralism, but a different form from yours. He speaks of the ultimate as a universal God who is 'a supreme reality of value, love and power',[15] 'a reality of compassion and bliss',[16] which is 'one, perfect, the cause of all'.[17] He does not actually specify that the ultimate is personal, although being loving, compassionate and blissful certainly seem to imply this. And he holds that the different major religions have different and partial glimpses of this God: 'virtually all serious religious traditions will contain matrices of myth which implicitly contain a disclosure of a reality of compassion and bliss which calls human beings to union with itself'.[18] Thus, he says, 'there is a spiritual reality of supreme power and value; but we are unlikely to have a very adequate conception of it'.[19] Does this seem right to you?

**John:**   Well, on the contemporary theological scene I see Ward as a major figure who is leading thought in entirely the right

[15]Keith Ward, 'Divine Ineffability' in *God, Truth and Reality*, op. cit., p. 218.
[16]Ibid.
[17]Ibid., p. 219.
[18]Ibid., p. 218.
[19]Ibid., p. 219.

direction. But you are right in thinking that my own position is more radical. It is also more comprehensive, in that it takes full account of the non-theistic as well as the theistic forms of religion – and indeed it is more radical precisely in order to be more comprehensive. I hold that the qualities which Ward attributes to God – value, love, compassion, power, bliss, unity, perfection – are elements in the rich conceptual repertoire with which we think, and hence experience, religiously. When the Real impinges upon our consciousness we can only experience in these and/or other comparable terms – such as just, judging, demanding, claiming, terrible, numinous, holy, awesome, etc. But all of these – even unity (and trinity) – are human concepts. If there is a reality beyond the range of our experience we have no reason to think that our system of experiential concepts applies to it; and if we regard the major religious traditions as humanly conditioned responses to such a reality we have a reason to think that these concepts do *not* apply to it – namely, as I pointed out just now, that if they did it would have mutually contradictory attributes, such as being personal and being non-personal, being a creator and not being a creator, and so on. So if, in view of their fruits in human life, you regard Buddhism, advaitic Hinduism, and Taoism, as well as the theistic faiths, as responses to the ultimate, you must postulate a reality to which these conceptual dualisms do not apply, although it is nevertheless humanly thought and experienced by means of them.

**Phil:**   So you don't accept that, as one critic says, 'the set of true propositions about a given image (e.g. Allah, or Amida Buddha) must form a subset of the set of all true propositions about the Eternal One [the Real] as it is in itself';[20] and you don't accept the description of the Real attributed to you by one critic as 'a reality of supreme love and power who will bring us all to final happiness in the end'.[21]

**John:**   No. This would be to forget the distinction between the Real in itself and its various experienceable personae, such as the

---

[20]Harold Netland, 'John Hick on Religious Pluralism', *Religious Studies*, Vol. 22, no. 2 (June 1986), p. 258.

[21]Keith Ward, 'Divine Ineffability', p. 216.

heavenly Parent of Jesus' teaching. The Real in itself cannot correspond to the anthropomorphic image of a powerful, loving being who acts in relation to us, bringing us to a happy fulfilment. But on the other hand we can properly speak mythologically of the Real in these – as also in many other, including non-personal – terms.

**Phil:**  But how then can the Real be worshipped? Surely an object of worship has to have some definite characteristics. It has to have a 'face' that we can recognize. As one critic asks, 'What could it possibly mean to worship a noumenon?'[22]

**John:**  What indeed? But of course we don't worship the noumenal Real in itself. We worship one or other of its personae – Allah, the Holy Trinity, Adonai, Vishnu, and so on. Or we orient ourselves in meditation towards one of its impersonae – the Tao, Brahman, the Dharma, Sunyata, and so on. But in doing so we are responding to the Real which, so to speak, lies behind its different manifestations to humankind.

**Phil:**  'Lying behind' being, I take it, a metaphor?

**John:**  Yes. What we're referring to in this way is the relationship between a reality as it is in itself, unperceived, and as it is perceived by a particular form of consciousness.

## The Real as vacuous and redundant

**Phil:**  OK. But that leads us to a related point. Various critics have pointed out that the concept of the Real as ineffable or formless constitutes the last stage in a movement from a more specific to a more general conception of the Ultimate. At one time, I believe, you spoke of the Ultimate as the triune God of Christianity; and then later as a kind of generic Deity, self-revealed through the different religions; but now finally as a Reality which is beyond both personality and impersonality and which indeed has no humanly thinkable attributes – other of course than the purely formal ones. And incidentally, as a small digression, some critics have made much of the fact that you've

---

[22]Eric O. Springsted, 'Conditions of Dialogue. John Hick and Simone Weil', *The Journal of Religion*, Vol. 72, no. 1 (January 1992), p.23.

changed your mind during the twenty or so years that you've been writing about this particular subject. Do you feel this as a criticism?

**John:**   Yes and no. Retrospectively, it implies a valid criticism of some of my earlier views. But in general I see it as a good sign if someone's perspective changes with continued reflection. I agree with Jonathan Swift when he said that 'A man should never be ashamed to own that he has been mistaken, which is but saying, in other words, that he is wiser today than he was yesterday'!

**Phil:**   OK. But concentrating on your wisdom of today, has not the Real, as the ultimate religious referent, now become in the words of one critic, 'so vague as to be entirely redundant'?[23] Have you not in fact, in the words of another critic, ended up in a 'transcendental agnosticism' [24]? Is not the Real a mere empty blank, such that it makes no difference whether it is there or not?

**John:**   I know that there are those who see this as an important criticism. But before answering it directly, let me remind you that I'm not saying that the Real does not have the nature that it has, but that this nature cannot be expressed within our human conceptual systems.

**Phil:**   So it does have attributes?

**John:**   Not if we mean by attributes distinguishable characteristics, because the very idea of an attribute in this sense is an element within our own conceptual schemas.

**Phil:**   So you're saying that the Real has its own nature, but that nature cannot be described in any human terms?

**John:**   Yes, if the Real is 'greater', or more than, or beyond, anything that we can conceive, this means that we cannot describe it with the concepts embodied in our human languages. But this is not to say that it is an empty blank. On the contrary,

---

[23]Brian Hebblethwaite, 'John Hick and the Question of Truth in Religion', in Arvind Sharma, (ed.), *God, Truth and Reality*, op. cit., p. 130.

[24]Gavin D'Costa, 'John Hick and Religious Pluralism: Yet Another Revolution' in Harold Hewitt, (ed.), *Problems in the Philosophy of Religion: Critical Studies of the Work of John Hick*, London: Macmillan and New York: St Martin's Press 1991, pp. 7f.

it is more than we can even imagine. As Anselm said, it is 'greater than we can conceive'.[25]

## So *why postulate the Real?*

**Phil:**   But then, since we can say nothing concrete about it, why suppose that it exists at all? What difference can its existence or nonexistence make? But I suppose you are going to say that 'existence' is also a human concept which does not apply here?

**John:**   Strictly speaking , yes – as was pointed some time ago now by Paul Tillich.[26] But we *can* ask, Why postulate the Real? Why, in that sense, suppose it to exist?

**Phil:**   OK. Why?

**John:**   In answering, can I assume that we share the basic faith that human religious experience is not purely projection and imagination but is a response to a transcendent reality of some kind?

**Phil:**   Yes, I think the critics I have in mind assume that.

**John:**   Well, if religion is a response, or a range of responses, what is it a response to? Christianity says the Holy Trinity; Islam, the strictly unitary Allah; Hinduism says that it is Brahman; and so on. But in regarding each of these, and the other major world traditions, as more or less equally effective contexts of salvation/ liberation, we are regarding them as responses to that to which religion is a response – which I am referring to as the Real.

**Phil:**   I suppose so.

**John:**   But in that case, can we say that one of these traditions is right in identifying the Real with, say, the Allah of Islam, and all the rest mistaken in identifying it with their own object of worship or focus of meditation?

**Phil:**   Well, don't people in each tradition do just that? Don't they each hold that their own awareness of the Ultimate is authentic whilst that of people within other traditions is mistaken or defective?

----

[25]Anselm, *Proslogion*, 15.

[26]Paul Tillich, *Systematic Theology*, Vol. I, Chicago: University of Chicago Press 1951 and London: SCM Press 1978, p. 205.

**John:**    Yes indeed. But this is where we came in! We started out
with the question whether confessional absolutism is consistent
with the recognition of the rough parity, so far as we can tell, of
the world religions as contexts of salvation/liberation. And
surely, if we take this parity seriously it is very implausible to
claim that only one of the salvific traditions, namely our own, has
a true conception of the Real. Would it not be more plausible to
suppose that the different objects of worship and foci of
contemplation are different manifestations of the ineffable Real-
in-itself? So the Real is that which there must be if human
religious experience, in its diversity of forms, is not purely
imaginary projection. It is, in Kantian terms, a necessary
postulate of religious experience in its diversity of forms.

**Phil:**    And yet on your view the different forms of religious
experience – experience of the trinitarian God, of Allah, of
Adonai, of Vishnu, of Shiva, and the experience of Brahman, of
the Dharmakaya, and so on – are all partly products of the human
imagination as it has been variously formed by the different
religio-cultural traditions?

**John:**    Yes. I'm applying to religious experience the epistemological principle that, in St Thomas' words, 'Things known are in
the knower according to the mode of the knower.'[27] This has
come to be known as critical realism. In distinction from naive
realism, which says that the world is just as it seems to us, critical
realism says that there is a real world around us but that we can
only know it as it appears to beings with our particular perceptual
machinery and conceptual resources. Thus critical realism takes
account of the difference made by the act of perception itself. And
applied to religion, it holds that there is a transcendent reality all
around and within and above and below us, but that we can only
know it in our own limited human ways. But I argued for this in
the first lecture, and you won't want me to repeat it again now.

**Phil:**    No. Some will have gone along with that, and others not.
But if one does accept it, how does it affect my question?

**John:**    Well, the difference between there being and there not
being a reality which is variously thought and experienced in the

---

[27] St Thomas, *Summa Theologiae*, II/II, Q. 1, art 2.

ways which the history of religions shows, is the difference between the truth of a naturalistic understanding of religion as purely human projection versus a critical realist understanding of it as a range of human, and therefore culturally conditioned, responses to a transcendent reality.

## But why only one Real?

**Phil:** But why *one* Real? Surely the fact that religion A points to an ineffable reality and that religion B points to an ineffable reality does not entitle you to infer that there is one ineffable reality to which they are both pointing. But several critics have taken this to be your reason for speaking of the Real in the singular. One says, 'Then he argues that, since one unknowable is indistinguishable from another, they are all the same'.[28] Another picks this up: 'Hick slips into the logical fallacy of the quantifier-shift when he adduces references to an ineffable reality in the sacred texts of the world's religions and deduces from this that they must all be referring to the same object, namely the Real'.[29] Are they right?

**John:** They're right of course that this would be an invalid argument, but wrong in attributing it to me. My reason to assume that the different world religions are referring, through their specific concepts of the Gods and Absolutes, to the same ultimate Reality is the striking similarity of the transformed human state described within the different traditions as saved, redeemed, enlightened, wise, awakened, liberated. This similarity strongly suggests a common source of salvific transformation. So it seems to me that the most reasonable hypothesis is that of a single ultimate ground of all human salvific transformation, rather than of a plurality of such grounds.

**Phil:** But still there *may* be a plurality of Reals.

**John:** Yes, we can't rule that out *a priori*. It wouldn't of course be a plurality of ultimates, because none of them would then be truly ultimate, but of penultimates. Or rather, we cannot rule out *a*

---

[28]Keith Ward, 'Truth and Religious Diversity', op. cit., p. 11. See also his *Religion and Revelation*, Oxford: Clarendon Press 1994, p. 313.

[29]Robert Cook, 'Postmodernism, pluralism and John Hick', op. cit., p. 11.

*priori* the possibility that there is nothing more ultimate than a co-existing plurality of personal deities, together with Brahman, the Tao, the Dharmakaya, Sunyata, and so on. But the problem with this picture is the difficulty of spelling out the relationship between these different realities. I suppose it's possible to think that Allah presides over Muslim countries, the Holy Trinity over Christian countries, Vishnu and Shiva over different parts of India, Adonai over Israel – but what about the still occupied territories? – and so on. But could one really make sense of this kind of polytheism, particularly today when people of different faiths are all mixed up together in so many areas? Or if we subsume all the God-figures under a single monotheistic deity, we still have the problem that if this deity is the creator of everything other than Godself, how can there be other equally ultimate non-personal realities? The Buddhist concept of the non-personal process of the universe, *pratitya samutpada*, precludes there being a God who is the universal creator. Some have suggested a single finite generic God together with just one of the non-personal absolutes.[30] But this would be a selective, and indeed arbitrarily selective, theory which it would be very hard to justify. And so there are great problems facing the idea of a plurality of ultimates. It does not seem to me a promising idea.

**Phil:**    And yet isn't it rather dogmatic to insist upon the oneness of the ultimate?

---

[30]This seems to be the position of John Cobb in 'Order Out of Chaos: A Philosophical Model of Inter-Religious Dialogue', in James Kellenberger, (ed.), *Inter-Religious Models and Criteria*, London: Macmillan, and New York: St Martin's Press 1993. See also Cobb's *Beyond Dialogue*, Philadelphia: Fortress Press 1982; 'Christian Witness in a Plural World' in *The Experience of Religious Diversity*, ed. John Hick and Hasan Askari (London, and Brookfield, Vermont: Gower 1985); and his 'Towards a Christocentric Catholic Theology' in Leonard Swidler, (ed.), *Towards a Universal Theology of Religion*, Maryknoll, New York: Orbis 1987. For a different but (to me) somewhat obscure kind of ultimate pluralism, see Raimundo Panikkar, 'The Jordan, the Tiber, and the Ganges' in *The Myth of Christian Uniqueness*, op.cit., and other writings, including 'The Invisible Harmony: A Universal Theory of Religion or a Cosmic Confidence in Reality?' in Leonard Swidler, (ed.), *Towards a Universal Theology of Religion*, op. cit.

**John:**   Well, strictly speaking we should not. For even number is part of our human conceptual repertoire. That which is ineffable, or formless, does not have number. But our language is such that we can only refer to the Real in either singular or plural terms. As Maimonides wrote, 'In our endeavour to show that God does not include a plurality, we can only say "He is one", although "one" and "many" are both terms which serve to distinguish quantity'.[31] In response to the same problem the Hindu scriptures speak of Brahman as 'The One without a second'. [32] So when we speak of *the* Real, this is not intended to say that the Real is one in distinction from two or three or more. The Real remains beyond the range of our human conceptuality, including the concept of number.

## Realism and eschatology

**Phil:**   Well, leaving that to our listeners, I'll move on now to yet another area. It has been said that your critical realism is cancelled by what you say about eschatology. You have distinguished between eschatologies, or concepts of the ultimate state, and pareschatologies, which are pictures of what happens between this life and that ultimate state.[33] You suggest that probably none of the pareschatologies of the different religions will turn out to be wholly true. And you say of the eschaton itself that it is probably beyond our present powers of conceiving or imagining. Some critics regard this as a rejection of realism. What about this?

**John:**   The question is whether agnosticism about the nature of the final state constitutes a non-realist use of eschatological language. And surely it does not. A non-realist understanding of eschatological language, such for example as that of D.Z. Phillips,[34] holds that there is no continued living after death and

---

[31]Moses Maimonides, *Guide for the Perplexed*, trans. M. Friedlander, 2nd ed., London: Routledge & Kegan Paul 1904, p. 81.

[32]*Chandogya Upanishad*, VI. 2. 2.

[33]John Hick, *Death and Eternal Life*, 1976, London: Macmillan 1985, and Louisville: Westminster/John Knox 1994.

[34]D.Z. Phillips, *Death and Immortality*, London: Macmillan 1970.

that talk of eternal life refers instead – for he assumes an exclusive
either/or at this point – to the quality of our present lives. In
contrast to this, I believe that there is indeed a final state, a
fulfilment of the project of human existence, beyond this life,
perhaps beyond many lives. However, I do not profess to know
what it is like.[35] But to hold that there is a presently unknown
final post-mortem state is quite different from holding that there
is no such state of any kind. Following the Buddha's teaching
about the 'undetermined questions', I also hold that we do not
need to know now the answer to these eschatological questions in
order to attain, or receive, the radically new state of existence
which constitutes salvation/liberation. But this does not constitute an anti-realist denial of eschatology.

**Phil:**    No, perhaps not; but in this same area a problem has also
been raised about eschatology and verifiability. Let me say first
that some have made much of differences between what you said
in *Death and Eternal Life* and what you say in *An Interpretation
of Religion*. Are there indeed these differences?

**John:**    Yes, in *Death and Eternal Life* (1976) I sided with
Ramanuja against Shankara in speculating about the ultimate
eschatological state. But in *An Interpretation* (1989) I had come
to think that we are not justified in making any descriptive
assertions about that ultimate state. But there were thirteen years
between the two books and I don't think that this growing
cautiousness has to be regarded as reprehensible – though it may
perhaps have something to do with increasing age!

**Phil:**    OK, but coming now to something more important, you
have always insisted that religious language not only functions to
order our thoughts and emotions, or to express our ruling ideals,
but also to refer to a transcendent reality or realities. It is used,
you say, not only to express but also to refer. And in support of
this you offered the idea of eschatological verification to show
that the reality of the transcendent is capable in principle of
experiential verification.[36]

---

[35] John Hick, *An Interpretation of Religion*, pp. 354–5.
[36] John Hick, *Faith and Knowledge*, 1957, 2nd ed. reissued, London:
Macmillan 1988, chs 7–8.

**John:** Yes, it seems to me clear that all the great world religions affirm that the nature or structure of the universe entails that future human experience will be different according to whether a religious or a naturalistic interpretation of it is correct. For the religions all teach that our present life is only a small part of our total existence. If, then, we find after our bodily death that we still exist, our experience will have falsified the naturalistic hypothesis.

**Phil:** Yes, I can accept that. And I can accept that if the eschatological beliefs of any one religion turn out to be true, they will be verified in future human experience – though I think this may be more clearly the case for the theistic than the non-theistic faiths. But how could the pluralistic hypothesis as a whole ever be experientially verified? As one critic has said, 'The question is whether there is an eschatological situation that would particularly confirm the terms of the pluralistic hypothesis itself "beyond a reasonable doubt". What specific state of affairs is predicted as confirmatory of the faith that there is a noumenal Real behind the specific religious traditions and that it is in relation to this Real that we are being salvifically transformed to a limitlessly better possibility?'[37]

**John:** This is a good question, in the sense of a difficult one! In responding I must begin with a distinction made in an earlier article in relation to theistic belief.[38] This is the distinction between, on the one hand, simple and direct, and on the other hand complex and indirect, verification. For example, 'There is a chair in the next room' can be verified by a single observation, whereas 'Jones is an honest man' can only be progressively confirmed in a series of observations spread out over time to the point at which there is no longer any reasonable doubt – this constituting, in such a case, verification. Now in traditional

---

[37]S. Mark Heim, 'The Pluralistic Hypothesis, Realism and Post-Eschatology', *Religious Studies*, Vol. 28, no. 2 (June 1992), p. 212. The problem is also raised by Gavin D'Costa in his chapter in *Problems in the Philosophy of Religion*, op. cit.

[38]John Hick, 'Eschatological Verification Reconsidered', *Religious Studies*, Vol. 13, no. 2 (June 1977), reprinted in *Problems of Religious Pluralism*, London: Macmillan and New York: St Martin's Press 1985.

theism God is defined as infinite, and hence incapable of being observed in any finite observation or series of observations. I therefore suggested that 'the proposition whose eschatological verification we should consider is not "God exists"; for this treats divine existence as an isolable and bounded fact. What we are seeking to verify is the truth of the theistic interpretation of the process of the universe, and this *verificandum* is embodied in a more complex proposition such as "The theistic account of the character of the universe, and of what is taking place in its history, is true" '.[39]

The same principal applies to the pluralistic hypothesis, only more so! There is no question of directly observing the Real *an sich*. What has to be progressively confirmed, to the exclusion of reasonable doubt, is that the pluralistic hypothesis fits the reported range of religious experience more fully and with greater conceptual economy than alternative hypotheses.

In this respect it is analogous to a large-scale scientific hypothesis – for example, the theory of evolution, or the expansion and the steady-state cosmologies. These cannot be decisively verified if true, but are nevertheless capable of being falsified if false. The most that can be required of such currently acceptable but falsifiable-if-false theories – and here I am of course following Karl Popper[40] – is that they fit the facts more comprehensively and more simply than alternative theories with the same domain. Thus biological evolution and the expansion of the universe stand up at present under this test, whereas the steady-state theory does not. In the religious domain the pluralistic hypothesis is proposed as the most comprehensive and economical theory, from a religious as distinguished from a naturalistic point of view, with which to understand the phenomena of religious experience. Like other large-scale theories it is not capable of direct experiential verification if true; but like any genuine theory it *is* capable of experiential falsification if false. This falsification would be eschatological. For example, if it turns

---

[39]John Hick, *Problems of Religious Pluralism*, op.cit., p. 116.

[40]Karl Popper, *The Logic of Scientific Discovery*, 1935, New York: Basic Books 1959.

out that any one of the rival belief-systems of the particular religions is true to the exclusion of the others, this would falsify the pluralistic hypothesis. To take a graphic example, if the Augustinian version of Christianity proves to be correct, and after a judgment by the risen Christ a small minority of men and women enjoy the presence of the Blessed Trinity whilst the large majority are consigned to the fires of hell, it will be evident that the pluralistic hypothesis was false!

**Phil:** OK. So you can say what, eschatologically, would falsify religious pluralism. But can you also say what, eschatologically, would *not* falsify it but on the contrary be cumulatively compatible with it and thus progressively confirm it?

**John:** Well, you can if you like create speculative post-mortem scenarios involving a future development in which at a certain point we can see in retrospect that the earthly religions were invaluable aids at an earlier stage, but have since been superseded in a more comprehensive vision. However, it is not necessary to produce such scenarios; and since they can be no more than speculations it seems to me better on the whole not to pursue that path.

**Phil:** So what path do you pursue instead?

**John:** A more holistic path. Remember that we are speaking from within the basic religious faith that religious experience is not purely projection but is at the same time our human response to a transcendent reality. I have expanded this in the light of the facts of religious diversity by saying that whilst its specific forms are provided by our different religious cultures, this mode of experience is also a cognitive response to the ultimate nature of reality. So within this expanded circle of faith I propose the hypothesis that the major different objects or contents of religious experience – Adonai, the Holy Trinity, Allah, Vishnu, Shiva, Brahman, Nirvana, the Tao, and so on – are manifestations to different forms of human consciousness of the ultimately real. This hypothesis, as an interpretation of the plurality of forms of religious experience, will be falsified if (*a*) the basic religious faith turns out to be correct but (*b*) this particular hypothesis about religious diversity turns out to be mistaken. It is thus a genuine hypothesis. It may be true; and I suggest that from our present vantage point it offers the best available religious explanation of the facts.

**Phil:**   So you are now at last abandoning, are you, the idea of verifiability as distinguished from falsifiability?

**John:**   Yes and no. Yes, in the sense that the Real, as the ultimate nature of reality, is not postulated as an entity that could ever be observed, even in a final eschatological state – so the idea of direct experiential verification does not apply here. But No, in the sense that the structure of reality, as it affects us human beings, can be progressively experienced and found to be such that the pluralistic hypothesis is the best picture of the universe that we can form – if, that is, it fits all the facts known to us and is not contradicted by the future development of our human experience.

## Criteria

**Phil:**   Well I'll leave that now and move to the question of criteria, which came up earlier and we postponed it. It came up when you said that a true myth is an *appropriate* response to the Real. Clearly there must be some criterion of appropriateness. Again, you say that we can criticize and sometimes utterly condemn aspects of each of the religions; and also that we can judge the great world faiths to be, as totalities, more or less equally effective contexts of salvation/liberation. But what criterion are you using when you say this, and where did you get it?

**John:**   I take the function of religion to be to facilitate what I have been calling salvation/liberation, meaning by this the transformation of human existence from self-centredness to a new centring in the Real – which of course means in practice the Real as known in a particular way within some particular tradition. And so the criterion by which to judge both a tradition as a whole and its constituent elements, including its doctrines, is soteriological. The question is how effectively they promote this salvific transformation.

**Phil:**   Right. So the question now is, how we can know when this transformation is taking place? You have said, by their fruits. But this is, in one writer's words, a 'pretty squashy criterion'![41]

---

[41]Ninian Smart in *God, Truth and Reality*, op. cit., p. 181.

**John:** Yes, I like that phrase! It's certainly a soft rather than a hard criterion, in that it does not deal in anything that can be precisely measured. But I think that in fact we all do use it. We wouldn't accept the religious credentials of a preacher or prophet or guru whom we see to be selfish, cruel, out to make money, or full of resentment and hatred. No one, for example, would think of Jesus as a son of God if they also thought that he was selfish, deceitful, exploitative and malicious. We all operate with an implicit or explicit moral criterion. Sam Keen vividly calls it our 'spiritual bullshit detector'.[42] It's not always easy to operate. But with care we can distinguish between phonies and individuals who are genuinely far advanced in the salvific transformation. They are the people (or rather some of the people) whom we call saints, jivanmuktas, arahats, bodhisattvas, mahatmas. And when we identify them we do so mainly by what are broadly ethical criteria.

**Phil:** '*Broadly* ethical'?

**John:** Well, some would prefer to use the term 'spiritual' for part of what I am calling 'ethical'. The people I regard as saints are strikingly unconcerned about themselves and are concerned instead to serve God or to live out the Dharma or the Tao or realize the universal Buddha nature, and we see in their lives an unselfish love and compassion that we all recognize as intrinsically valuable, indeed often awe-inspiringly so.

**Phil:** Yes, but how do you know that love and compassion are, to use your own word, the *appropriate* response to the Real?

**John:** Because all of the great traditions teach this, and I am taking them to be authentic responses to the Real. They all teach the ideal of seeking the good of others as much as of oneself. For example, from Buddhism, 'As a mother cares for her son, all her days, so towards all living things a man's mind should be all-embracing';[43] from Hinduism, 'One should never do that to another which one regards as injurious to one's own self. This, in brief, is the rule of Righteousness';[44] from Confucianism, 'Do not

---

[42]Sam Keen, *Hymns to an Unknown God*, New York and London: Bantam Books 1994, pp. 110f.

[43]*Sutta Nipata*, 149.

[44]*Mahabharata*, Anushana parva, 113.7.

do to others what you would not like yourself';[45] from Taoism, the good man 'will regard [others'] gains as if they were his own, and their losses in the same way';[46] from Christianity, 'As ye would that men should do to you, do ye also to them likewise';[47] from Judaism, 'What is hateful to yourself do not do to your fellow man. This is the whole of the Torah';[48] and from Islam, 'No man is a true believer unless he desires for his brother that which he desires for himself'.[49]

**Phil:** OK. But haven't you now spun a circular argument?[50] You start with the assumption that these various traditions are authentic responses to the Real, and then you use their moral teachings as the criterion by which to judge that they *are* authentic responses to the Real! Isn't this clearly a vicious circle?

**John:** It's a circle, I agree, but it's the kind of circle which *any* comprehensive view inevitably involves. If you hold, for example, a naturalistic view of the universe you have to use naturalistic assumptions to support it. Or if you hold that Christianity is the only true faith you will inevitably be using its own special criteria to establish this. There are no non-circular ways of establishing fundamental positions.

**Phil:** That sounds to me rather theoretical. Can you make it a bit more convincing?

**John:** Well, let me put it another way. In offering a religious as distinguished from a naturalistic interpretation of religion I'm speaking from within the circle of religious faith, not professing to establish the validity of that faith. And I don't mean here a tradition-specific faith but the basic conviction, common to all the great traditions, that religious experience is not simply human projection but is at the same time a cognitive response to a transcendent reality which is of limitless importance to us. There's an implicit criterion at work here, for within this basic

[45]*Analects*, XII. 2.

[46]*Thai Shang*, 3.

[47]Luke 6. 31.

[48]*Babylonian Talmud*, Shabbath 31a.

[49]Hadith, *Muslim*, chapter on *iman*, 71–2.

[50]See, e.g., Timothy R. Stinnett, 'John Hick's Pluralistic Theory of Religion', *The Journal of Religion*, Vol. 70, no. 4 (October 1990). p. 586.

faith one does not regard *all* forms of religion, including for example Satanism or the Jonestown and Waco movements, as authentic responses to the Real. I think it's clear that this implicit criterion focusses upon observable 'fruits' in human life. This criterion is integral to the basic religious faith, and this faith as a whole constitutes a circle in the sense that it cannot be independently established.

Let me just add the familiar analogy to this in our normal acceptance of our ordinary sense experience. We live all the time by faith in the cognitive character of sense perception, and this faith includes implicit criteria by which we distinguish between genuine perceptions on the one hand and hallucinations, dreams, illusions on the other. But there is no non-circular way of showing that sense perception, as defined by these criteria, is indeed veridical, since any evidence that we appeal to must consist in other moments of sense perception. This kind of circularity is simply unavoidable, whether in relation to sense or to religious experience.

### Social salvation/liberation

**Phil:**   Well, I'll leave that to our listeners. But now something else occurs to me. You've been speaking about salvation/liberation mainly in individual terms. But what about societies? After all, we are not isolated units but always members both of a local society and of the world-wide society of humankind.

**John:**   Yes, and it's one of the sad facts of life that goodness and love are much less easily built into enduring social structures than selfishness and greed. Reinhold Niebuhr pointed to this when he spoke of 'moral man and immoral society'.[51] But there's been an interesting development in the typical forms of saintliness in recent decades. In earlier ages the great economic and political structures were regarded as givens, like the landscape or the climate, and were seen as ultimately ordained by God. And so saintliness usually had to take purely personal forms, including

---

[51]Reinhold Niebuhr, *Moral Man and Immoral Society*, New York: Charles Scribner's Sons 1941 and Edinburgh: T. & T. Clark 1980.

acts of individual charity. But beginning with the work of Karl Marx in the nineteenth century, what we can call a sociological consciousness has developed and has now become general. We know that these structural circumstances can be analysed, understood, and purposefully changed. And so the more typical form of saintliness today is political. As Harvey Cox has said, 'the world has taken the place of the wilderness as the classical testing ground for sanctity and purification'.[52] The greatest political saint of our century was, surely, Gandhi, for whom the service of Truth – by which he did not mean propositional truths but *sat*, the Real – included both the inner transformation of individuals and the outer transformation of society by non-violent means, first in South Africa and then in India. We think also of Martin Luther King in this country, and of Archbishop Romero in El Salvador, and Dom Helda Camara in Brazil, and other practitioners of liberation theology in South America, and of Nelson Mandela and Desmond Tutu in South Africa; and of many, many others who have given and are giving their energies, and sometimes their lives, in working for justice and peace on earth. This is the typically contemporary form taken by the transformation of human beings from self-centredness to a new orientation centred in the Transcendent.

**Phil:**   Despite the fact that many who are giving their time and energies in this way are non-religious? After all, many – it might even turn out to be the majority – are either humanists or Marxists. Are they then also responding to the Real, but without knowing it?

**John:**   Yes, from a religious point of view they are. They feel the presence of the Real in the call of conscience to work against exploitation, against racism, against poverty and starvation, and to work for the creation of justice and peace on earth.[53]

---

[52]Harvey Cox in *Our Religions*, ed. Arvind Sharma, New York: HarperCollins 1993, p. 392.

[53]Duncan Forrester has complained that my position implies 'that there is no salvation outside religion' ('Professor Hick and the Universe of Faiths', *Scottish Journal of Theology*, Vol. 29, no. 1, February 1976, p. 70). But surely there is no such implication.

**Phil:**   So you include those who do not believe that there is any transcendent reality such as the religions speak of, but who nevertheless work unselfishly for a better human future, among those who are responding in their lives to the Real and are undergoing the salvific transformation. It seems to me that you are a kind of inclusivist after all!

**John:**   And why not? But of course to have an inclusivist view in one area does not mean that one must also have an inclusivist view in another. Each issue has to be considered on its own merits.

**Phil:**   Well thank you for these responses. Some of our hearers will have been persuaded by them, and some not. But now I'm going to pass the torch to Grace, who will be raising more theological questions.

# 4

# Incarnation and Uniqueness

## Summary so far

**John:** Last time I was discussing with Phil the possibility of a religious interpretation of religion across the centuries and around and the world. I suggested that if this is not simply to fit the other major faiths into the framework of one's own, it must speak of an ultimate transcendent reality which is the ground and source of everything, but which in its inner nature lies beyond the scope of our human conceptual systems. This reality (which I have been referring to as the Real) is differently conceived, and therefore differently experienced, and therefore differently responded to from within the different world religions. Phil put forward various philosophical objections to this hypothesis, and we discussed these. And now, I believe, we're going to discuss a different set of problems.

**Grace:** Yes, I'm interested in the more theological criticisms that have been made of this idea. Of course, there's inevitably some overlap with the philosophical issues, but so far as possible we'll be taking up new questions. And we're speaking now, aren't we, within the circle of specifically Christian faith?

**John:** Yes, though of course in my view Christian faith cannot be a closed circle that we can inhabit whilst ignoring everything outside. We have to do theology today in the context of the world as it is, including our new awareness of the other great world faiths.

## 'Outside the church, no salvation'

**Grace:** Yes, though whether this theological method is allowable may prove to be a major issue in its own right. But let's look at specific criticisms that have been made. Generally the critics are reacting against the implications of the pluralistic hypothesis, particularly for the central doctrines of Incarnation, Trinity and Atonement. But before that, I'd like to take up a different point. This concerns the Catholic dogma, *extra ecclesiam nulla salus*, 'outside the church, no salvation'. You've quoted the pronouncement of Pope Boniface VIII in 1302: 'We are required by faith to believe and hold that there is one holy, catholic and apostolic church; we firmly believe it and unreservedly profess it; outside it there is neither salvation nor remission of sins . . . Further, we declare, say, define and proclaim that to submit to the Roman Pontiff is, for every human creature, an utter necessity of salvation',[1] and the decree of the Council of Florence in 1438–45 that 'no one remaining outside the Catholic Church, not just pagans, but also Jews or heretics or schismatics, can become partakers of eternal life; but they will go to the "everlasting fire which was prepared for the devil and his angels," unless before the end of life they are joined to the Church',[2] and you've understood these dogmatic formulations to mean that non-Christians go to hell.

John:    Yes indeed. I added of course that 'The Roman Catholic Church today has passed decisively beyond this phase',[3] citing particularly the second Vatican Council in the 1960s. But the old dogma that non-Christians go to hell is still, alas, alive in extreme Protestant fundamentalist circles. You've probably read the message of the Congress on World Mission at Chicago in 1960, which declared, 'In the years since the war [i.e. since 1945], more than one billion souls have passed into eternity and more than half of these went to the torment of hell fire without even hearing of Jesus Christ, who He was, or why He died on the cross of Calvary'.[4]

---

[1] Denzinger, *Enchirdion Symbolorum*, no. 468.

[2] Denzinger, no. 714.

[3] John Hick, *God Has Many Names*, Philadelphia: Westminster Press, 1982, p. 30.

[4] *Facing the Unfinished Task*, ed. J.O. Percy, Grand Rapids, Michigan: Eerdmans 1961, p. 9. For a recent discussion of different evangelical views of the fate of the unconverted see W. Gary Phillips, 'Evangelicals and Pluralism: Current Options' in *Proceedings of the Wheaton College Theology Conference*, Vol. 1 (Spring 1991).

**Grace:** But does anyone think like that today ?

**John:** Yes, I'm afraid so. A prominent evangelical Christian philosopher says that 'If we take scripture seriously, we must admit that the vast majority of persons in the world are condemned and will be forever lost, even if in some relatively rare cases a person might be saved through his response to the light that he has apart from revelation'.[5] He seeks to reconcile this with the infinite divine love by suggesting that, because God has 'middle knowledge', i.e., knows what everyone *would* do in all possible circumstances, 'If there were anyone who would have responded to the gospel if he had heard it, then God in His love would have brought the gospel to such a person . . . God in His providence has so arranged the world that as the gospel spread outward from its historical roots in first-century Palestine, all who would respond to this gospel, were they to hear it, did and do hear it.'[6]

**Grace:** You mean, God knows, concerning all the millions of people who have not heard the gospel, that if they *did* hear it they would reject it – and so it's right and just for them to go to hell ?

**John:** Yes, apparently so. Craig says, 'God in His providence has so arranged the world that anyone who would receive Christ has the opportunity to do so'.[7] So God knew concerning the hundreds of millions of men, women and children in China and India and Africa and Australasia and the rest of the world before the modern missionary movement that each one of them would have rejected the gospel if they had heard it! But can one really, simply on the basis of the fact that they did not hear the Christian gospel, declare that all these millions of men and women deserved to go to eternal hell ? Is this not *a priori* dogmatism of the most blindly insensitive kind ?

**Grace:** Yes, I have to agree with you there. But returning to the Catholic *extra ecclesiam* doctrine, this did not prevent the church from presuming the salvation of the patriarchs of the Old

[5]William Lane Craig, ' "No Other Name": a Middle Knowledge Perspective on the Exclusivity of Salvation through Christ', *Faith and Philosophy*, Vol. 6, no. 2 (April 1989), p. 176. See also Vol. 8, no. 3 (July 1991) and Vol. 10, no, 2 (April 1993).

[6]Ibid., p. 185.       [7]Ibid, p. 186.

Testament, who were obviously not members of the visible church. The essential point of the dogma, surely, is that 'all grace, and thereby salvation, is related to Christ and thereby to his church'.[8] But that salvific power of Christ extends beyond the circle of those who explicitly know him. Further, the early church often had a more generous outlook towards non-Christians than the mediaeval church whose pronouncements you quoted.[9] Would you accept this?

**John:** Yes, there was a much more open and experimental phase of Christian thinking before church and empire combined and imposed a rigid orthodoxy.

**Grace:** Further, it's claimed by some that the *extra ecclesiam* dogma was not intended to address the question of non-Christian religions as such at all. Would you accept that also?

**John:** There's a sense in which that must be so, in that our modern concept of a religion, as a socio-religious entity over against other such entities, had not yet developed – as Wilfred Cantwell Smith has shown in his classic study *The Meaning and End of Religion*.[10] But it certainly *was* directed against the *people* of those religions. Pope Boniface spoke of '*every* human creature' as having to become a Christian as 'an utter necessity of salvation'; and the Council of Florence spoke of pagans, which meant non-Christians (other than Jews) generally,[11] as well as Jews and Christian heretics and schismatics, as destined for hell. So I don't think it is possible to evade the horrific implication of

---

[8]Gavin D'Costa, in Ian Hamnett (ed.), *Religious Pluralism and Unbelief*, London and New York: Routledge 1990, p. 130.

[9]E.g., 'Those who live according to the Logos are Christians, notwithstanding they may pass with you for atheists; such among the Greeks were Socrates and Herakleitos. . .' (Justin Martyr, *First Apology*, 46); 'What is now called the Christian religion, has existed among the ancients, and was not absent from the beginning of the human race, until Christ came in the flesh; from which time the true religion, which existed already, began to be called Christian' (St Augustine, *Retractions*, 1, 13).

[10]Wilfred Cantwell Smith, *The Meaning and End of Religion* (1962), London: SPCK and Minneapolis: Fortress Press 1991.

[11]The *Oxford English Dictionary* cites fifteenth century writers, contemporary with the Council of Florence, who meant by pagans people with a false, i.e. non-Christian, religion.

the mediaeval dogma, even though it was not framed in the context of our contemporary debates.

**Grace:** Well, as an attempt to evade what you call its horrific implication one writer has said that, 'Heretics, schismatics, and Jews belonged to one category – those who had properly heard of and rejected Christ, each in a different manner. In this sense it was clear to the Fathers that for those "outside the church" there was no salvation. Later, it has also become clear that this was not primarily a personal judgment upon the fate of anyone, – and the axiom could therefore be seen as a grammatical rule, not a condemnatory proposition'.[12] Does this help ?

**John:** Well first, we must not forget the 'pagans', who would include Buddhists, Hindus, Jains, Zoroastrians, Taoists, Confucianists, and the people of the primal religions. Whether it would include Muslims, or whether these would come under the heading of heretics (for Muhammad was regarded by some as a Christian apostate), is a moot point; but either way they are condemned to hell along with the rest, in their tens of millions. And it would be little consolation to Jews, or to Christian heretics and schismatics, as they burn in hell, that the Council's Decree was only a grammatical rule! If I were a Catholic I would let the old *extra ecclesiam* formula pass quietly into the museum of defunct dogmas rather than revive it today by trying to defend it. It is a profoundly unhappy formulation, surely now best forgotten.

**Grace:** I'll leave that to our Catholic friends. But now let's come to the implications of religious pluralism. These implications are, wouldn't you agree, pretty drastic?

**John:** Yes, at least in relation to the traditional structure of Christian theology.

**Grace:** Well, to start with incarnation, what problem do you find with this?

### Christianity's claim to unique superiority

**John:** The doctrine of the incarnation, as it's traditionally understood, tells us – doesn't it? – that the historical individual,

---

[12]Gavin D'Costa, in *Religious Pluralism and Unbelief*, op.cit., pp. 135–6.

Jesus of Nazareth, was God the Son, the second person of a divine Trinity, incarnate. He was both fully and genuinely a man and fully and genuinely God, and as such he had two natures, one human and the other divine. This leads, in my view, straight to the assumption, which I was questioning in my lecture, of the unique superiority of Christianity. The incarnation doctrine entails that the Christian religion, alone among the religions of the world, was founded by God in person — for it's part of traditional orthodoxy both that there has been only one incarnation, and that Jesus, who was God incarnate, instituted the Christian church. And it seems obvious that having come to earth to found a new religion God must intend it to supersede all other religions and to embrace the entire human race. But clearly this is incompatible with a pluralist understanding of Christianity as one salvific response among others to the ultimate reality that we call God.

**Grace:**  True. But various people have suggested ways in which we can still hold that Jesus was God incarnate and yet not claim superiority for Christianity; and I think we ought to look at these. I suppose you would at least agree that a traditionally orthodox Christian does not have to adopt an arrogant or dismissive attitude to people of other religions? Surely he or she can hold them in high regard, can love them, can have great respect for them, can dialogue courteously with them, can learn from them, can see them as no less truly children of God than are Christians.

**John:**  Yes of course; and many do. I'm not talking about personal attitudes, but about the logic of beliefs. It seems to me that the belief that Christianity alone among the religions of the world was founded by God in person entails its unique superiority, even though many Christians may politely refrain from saying so in their dealings with Jews, Muslims, Hindus, Buddhists, and so on. So what are the ways of avoiding this implication that you have in mind?

**Grace:**  There are several, all variations on the theme of the Logos, the Word of God, which is universally at work seeking to bring men and women to God. They hold that the Logos, which became incarnate as Jesus Christ, is active within other religions in different but no less valuable ways, so that Christianity is not necessarily superior to those other religions.

**John:**   I think this needs to be spelled out. What exactly do they have in mind?

**Grace:**   The strongest version – which I've not seen in print though I've sometimes heard it in discussion – is the idea of a plurality of divine incarnations. After all, no less a theologian than Thomas Aquinas argued that this is theoretically possible[13] – although this has never, so far as I know, been taken up in orthodox theology. But presumably it would mean that the Logos became incarnate not only as Jesus of Nazareth but also as the founders of the other great world religions, or at least some of them.

**John:**   You mean such figures as Abraham and Moses, and Gautama the Buddha, and Muhammad?

**Grace:**   Yes, though probably many Christians, with our tremendous load of inherited prejudice and misinformation about the prophet of Islam, would find it difficult to think of him as a divine incarnation.

**John:**   And of course Muhammad himself would certainly have regarded the idea as blasphemous.

**Grace:**   Yes; but at any rate the list might have to include those four and perhaps also Lao-Tzu, the founder of Taoism, and Mahavira the founder of Jainism, and Guru Nanak the founder of Sikhism . . . but just how far it would go is a good question. Would it include Shinran, founder of Amida Buddhism, Joseph Smith, founder of Mormonism, Mary Baker Eddy, founder of Christian Science, the Rev. Sun Myung Moon, founder of the Unification Church, and so on? To specify the divine incarnations would, I suspect, prove embarassingly difficult. So I'm not pressing this option.

**John:**   I think you're wise. But apart from that difficulty there's still the more fundamental problem, which we must come to presently, of giving concrete meaning to the idea that *any* historical individual is both literally a human being and literally God.

**Grace:**   Yes, but that cuts in more than one direction. There are other religions as well as Christianity that speak of divine incarnations – from Palaeolithic incarnations of spirits pictured

---

[13] St Thomas, *Summa Theologiae*, Part IIa, Q 3–4.

in a Trois Freres cave, to shamanite incarnations of divine beings, ancient Iranian expectations of an incarnation of Mithra, the ancient Egyptian and Japanese belief that the king was God incarnate, the Buddhist conception of the historical Siddhartha Gautama as an incarnation of a heavenly Buddha, and the Hindu belief in the many incarnations of Vishnu, the list of which seems fairly open.[14] (In modern times Sri Ramakrishna has been regarded by many Hindus as such an incarnation, and more recently Mahatma Gandhi.) Presumably if the idea of an historical individual being fully human and fully divine is incoherent, this will apply outside Christianity also?

**John:** Yes, of course. Though in fact I don't think that either the Hindu doctrine of the many *avatars* of Vishnu, or the Mahayana trikaya doctrine according to which the heavenly Buddhas of the *sambhogakaya* become incarnate as the earthly Buddhas of the *nirmanakaya,* involve a two natures concept such as the church adopted at Chalcedon. But certainly the argument that such a Chalcedonian-type doctrine is incoherent will apply outside Christianity as well as within.

**Grace:** Any way, no one in the Christian world seems to be pressing the plural incarnations idea. A less dramatic conception focusses on the universal activity of the Holy Spirit or of the divine Logos as inspiring the great religious figures of other traditions, and their ordinary adherents also so far as they are open to such inspiration. So one writer says that the doctrine of the Trinity 'facilitates an openness to the world religions, for the activity of the Spirit cannot be confined to Christianity',[15] whilst another variation on the theme is that 'God through Christ operates from within their traditions [i.e. "most non-Christian traditions"] and draws all towards himself'.[16]

**John:** And this is held to be *as* religiously valuable as the incarnation of the Logos as Jesus Christ?

---

[14]See, e.g., 'Incarnation' in the *Encyclopedia of Religion*, ed. Mircea Eliade, Vol. 7, New York: Macmillan and London: Collier Macmillan 1987.

[15]Gavin D'Costa, in *Christian Uniqueness Reconsidered*, op. cit., p. 17.

[16]Julius Lipner, 'Does Copernicus Help?', *Religious Studies*, Vol. 13, no. 2 (June 1977), p. 258.

**Grace:**  Perhaps not, because the former writer goes on to say that 'the God who redeems is always and everywhere the triune God revealed in Christ'[17] and that 'Jesus is the *normative* criterion for God, while not foreclosing the ongoing self-disclosure of God in history, through the Spirit.'[18] And the latter says, 'We may well be permitted to speak of the unknown Christ of Hinduism, and still express our firm commitment to him as the definitive focus of an unveiling of the inscrutable God he called Father'.[19]

**John:**  So it seems that the Christian revelation is still normative and in that sense superior to all others. But is this surprising? Musn't this be true in the end for all forms of Christian inclusivism, even when their advocates are anxious to conceal it?

**Grace:**  But I find that inclusivists usually don't like the word 'superior' in this context.

**John:**  No, and I don't blame them; but in that case shouldn't they abandon the dogma that entails it? It's also true that some Christian absolutists are now beginning to call themselves 'Christian particularists'[20] instead, in an attempt to shed the unattractive older image. This is a good sign; but it hasn't yet altered the substance of what they say, or the implications of that substance.

## Incarnation

**Grace:**  All right. So let's get now directly to the Incarnation doctrine. I must first confront you with Jesus' own claim: 'I and the Father are one' (John 10.30), 'He who has seen me has seen the Father' (John 14.9).

**John:**  Yes, and at this point we're in danger of falling into the bottomless pit of biblical criticism! I'm not myself primarily a biblical scholar and I rely mainly on the work of the full-time

---

[17]D'Costa, ibid., p. 17.

[18]D'Costa, ibid, p. 23.

[19]Lipner, 'Does Copernicus Help?', p. 257.

[20]E.g. Alister McGrath, 'A Particularist Approach' in, *More Than One Way?* ed. Dennis Ockholm and Timothy Phillips, Grand Rapids, Michigan: Zondervan 1995.

professionals. But I think it's safe to say that there's a general consensus in New Testament studies today, Catholic as well as Protestant, conservative as well as liberal, that the historical Jesus, did not teach that he was God, or God the Son, the second person of a Holy Trinity, incarnate. Indeed he would probably have regarded such an idea as blasphemous! One of the sayings attributed to him is, 'Why do you call me good? No one is good but God alone' (Mark 10.18). He most probably thought of himself as the final prophet, sent by God to proclaim the imminent coming of God's kingdom on earth and to prepare Israel for this. He may – but on the other hand he may very possibly not – have thought of himself as the messiah or as the Danielic son of man who was to appear on the clouds of heaven; though the Jesus movement after his death, and after the event that we call his resurrection, adopted both of these ideas and eventually fused them together. But we have to remember that none of the Gospel writers was among Jesus' original twelve disciples and that they were writing forty to seventy years after his death, using stories about him which had undergone a considerable process of selection, adaptation and development in the intervening period. In the case of the great 'I am' sayings I don't think any reputable scholar today would maintain that these are words of the historical Jesus. The Fourth Gospel is generally thought to have been written towards the end of the first century and to express the theology that had developed in this writer's part of the church. It is this Johannine and Pauline theology that was to become Christian orthodoxy – which is of course why it dominates the New Testament canon that the church eventually adopted. But nevertheless it does not reflect Jesus' own self-understanding so far as scholars have been able to reconstruct this from the synoptic and the extra-canonical Gospels.

**Grace:** Well if Jesus was not the Second Person of the Holy Trinity living a human life, who or what was he?

## *Jesus as a Spirit-filled man*

**John:** In my view, he was unambiguously a man, but a man who was open to God's presence to a truly awesome extent and was sustained by an extraordinarily intense God-consciousness. It was this that made God real to others and revolutionized the lives of many who met him, summoning them to live in the way that is natural in God's presence, a life of trust and love, and of healing and peace-making in a broken world. If you or I had met Jesus in first-century Galilee what would have struck us most, I believe, would have been both his tremendous spiritual authority and his tremendous accepting love, challenging and calling and enabling us to enter this new life. We wouldn't, as first-century Jews, have thought for a moment that he was Jahweh, or a trinitarian God the Son, though we might very well have thought of him in the familiar Hebraic metaphor as a son of God. For we would have recognized that he was very much closer to God than ourselves and we would, I hope, have responded by taking him as our lord, or in Eastern terms our guru, the one whom we follow and obey.

**Grace:**   This is how you picture him. But can you really be sure that this is how he actually was?

**John:**   No, I can't. And neither can anyone else be sure that he was as they picture him. The entire history of New Testament study shows that the material is always open to a range of varying interpretations. Every picture of Jesus is necessarily based upon a selection from the data. And my own picture is based on my own selection, guided by many factors, including my knowledge of some spiritually very impressive individuals and my reading about others.

**Grace:**   But if Jesus was an ordinary, or rather an extraordinary, human being, what do you think was the message that he preached?

**John:**   He seems to have shared the eschatological strand of thought within the Judaism of his time, believing in the imminent end of the present age and the coming of God's kingdom; and he was seeking to prepare Israel for this. According to Mark's Gospel, 'Jesus came into Galilee, preaching the gospel of God, and saying, "The time is fulfilled, and the kingdom of God is at hand; repent, and believe in the gospel"' – the gospel of God being the good news that the kingdom was at hand (Mark 1.15). Again according to Mark he said 'Truly, I say to you, there are some standing here who will not taste death before they see that the kingdom of God has come with power' (Mark 9.1). And the early Jesus movement waited in urgent expectation for their lord to appear again to inaugurate the kingdom.[21] But as this expectation gradually faded during the succeeding decades he was transformed in the mind of the church from the eschatological prophet of Israel into a semi-divine Son of God and then eventually into the fully divine God the Son, second person of the Holy Trinity.

## 'Son of God'

**Grace:**   You imply a development in the son of God idea.

**John:**   Yes. The starting point lies in the fact that outstanding human beings, particularly kings and emperors and pharaohs, but also great philosophers and holy men, were often referred to in the ancient Near East as sons of God or as divine men or even as gods. And indeed the term 'son of God' was as much in use in ancient Judaism as in the wider world.

**Grace:**   In Judaism also?

**John:**   Yes indeed. In the Hebrew scriptures Israel as a whole is called God's son (Hos. 11.1). Angels are called sons of God (Job 38.7). And the ancient Israelite kings were enthroned as son of God. We have what is probably the enthronement formula, 'You are my son, today I have begotten you', in Psalm 2.7. But in terms of our modern distinction this language was clearly metaphorical. No one thought that king David, for example, of whom God said, 'I will be his father, and he shall be my son' (II Sam. 7.14), was literally begotten by God. And in Luke's Gospel Jesus' genealogy goes back to 'Adam, the son of God' (Luke 3.38). But, more broadly, any outstandingly pious individual among the children of Israel, down to Jesus' time and beyond, could be referred to metaphorically as a son of God. So, yes, Jesus was certainly a son of God in the familiar metaphorical sense that was prevalent in the world of his time.

---

[21]E.g. Paul characterized as 'the word of the Lord' the promise that those who are alive when the Lord returns will not precede [into heaven] those who have already died (I Thess. 4.15).

**Grace:** And do you think he thought of himself in this way?
**John:** I would think very probably so. After all, he called God *Abba*, and taught his followers to do the same. But we have to remember what this language meant in the world of Jesus' time. A fairly conservative New Testament scholar, James Dunn, writing about Christian origins asks, 'What would it have meant to their hearers when the first Christians called Jesus "son of God"? All the time [he says] in a study like this we must endeavour to attune our listening to hear with the ears of the first Christians' contemporaries. We must attempt the exceedingly difficult task of shutting out the voices of early Fathers, Councils and dogmaticians down the centuries, in case they drown the earlier voices, in case the earlier voices were saying something different, in case they intended their words to speak with different force to their hearers.'[22] And in Jesus' world to refer to him as 'son of God' did not imply that he was literally God's son, with divine sperm entering his mother's ovum at his conception – although the virgin birth story in Matthew and Luke does, at any rate to a modern reader, come perilously close to this. The term 'son of God' was not intended literally but as metaphor, indicating that he was close to God, open to God's presence, doing God's will. It was only later, in the different context of the Gentile world, that the familiar metaphor was transformed into a metaphysical doctrine.
**Grace:** So what happened?
**John:** The history in its fullness is complex and open, at various points, to different interpretations. It's been told in a number of excellent recent books such as, for example, Paula Fredricksen's *From Jesus to Christ.*[23] But reducing it to its bare bones, when the church went out into the Gentile world and Christianity became, in the fourth century, the official religion of the Roman Empire, its beliefs were recast in the Greek philosophical terms that constituted the intellectual language of the time, and the meta-

---

[22]James D. G. Dunn, *Christology in the Making: An Inquiry into the Origins of the Doctrine of the Incarnation*, London: SCM Press and Philadelphia: Westminster Press 1980, pp. 13–14.
[23]Paula Fredricksen, *From Jesus to Christ*, New Haven: Yale University Press 1988.

phorical son of God became the metaphysical God the Son, second person of a divine Trinity, incarnate in two natures, one human and the other divine. This was what was decided at the councils of Nicaea in 325 and Chalcedon in 451, and it's remained official Christian doctrine ever since.

**Grace:** And yet you want to deny this?

**John:** Yes, I'm one of a large number of theologians today who want to leave Nicaea and Chalcedon behind as documents of their own time which are no longer helpful to us today.

**Grace:** Why?

### A God who does not know that he is God

**John:** I think there are three main problems with the traditional doctrine. We've already noted one: the fact that it was not taught by Jesus himself but is a creation of the church. You see, the realization that Jesus did not teach his own divinity is – with a few exceptions – quite modern, arising from the critical-historical study of Christian origins during about the last century and a half. But it would have been regarded as literally damnable heresy at the time when what we now know as Christian orthodoxy was established. For example, the Council of Chalcedon declared of its doctrine of Jesus as 'Son and Only-begotten God the Word' that this was 'as . . . our Lord Jesus Christ himself taught us'. However, we now have good reason to think that he taught no such thing.

**Grace:** But don't you think that the modern church as a whole has nevertheless come to accept the main results of New Testament research?

**John:** Yes, generally speaking it has; but often without fully facing their implications. Have we really come to terms with the paradox of God incarnate who doesn't know that he is God incarnate? This provokes the question, How can the church claim to know who Jesus was better than he knew himself? The paradox is heightened by the realization that Jesus cannot have intended to found a church, or a new religion outside Judaism, if he expected, as he and his early followers seem to have done, the end of the present age within a few years or perhaps even months. So we owe the creation of Christianity, not to Jesus, but to the spiritual needs and propensities of those who were moved and changed by his influence. This charismatic man, filled with the divine Spirit, was gradually exalted and magnified by human piety into the pre-existent Christ, the eternal Logos, by whom all things were made and by whom all things are ruled. But after the discovery that Jesus himself did not teach any of this we need other reasons to continue to believe it today and to hold that it is the full and final truth for all humankind.

**Grace:**   But even if Jesus himself did not actually teach that he was God incarnate, did he not *imply* it by the divine authority that he assumed in abrogating the Jewish Law and in forgiving sins? Surely his deity is implicit even if not explicit in his life and teaching?

**John:**   Here we enter again the realm of the conflicting theories of biblical scholarship. I agree that it's possible to see an implicit claim to deity here. But on the other it is equally possible to see the material quite differently. It has often been said that Jesus assumed a divine authority in cancelling aspects of the Jewish Law. But a strong stream of contemporary New Testament research today, exphasizing the Jewishness of Jesus, holds that he did not in fact abrogate the Law. I would refer you, for example, to the work of E.P. Sanders in *Jesus and Judaism*[24] and other books. Again, Sanders and many others hold that in pronouncing forgiveness for sins Jesus was, out of his vivid awareness of God's mercy, declaring God's forgiveness, not presuming himself to be God. But it must be said that these are questions which the New Testament scholars will probably debate among themselves until the end of time. And I think you will notice that their interpretations are invariably correlated with their wider theological positions. If you want biblical confirmation for a conservative position, you can find it, and if you want biblical confirmation for a more liberal position you can find that. This is admittedly disconcerting if we had thought that we can settle our theological problems from the Bible. But the situation is really the other way round: we all use the Bible selectively (whether consciously or not) in the light of our theological outlook.

---

[24]E.P. Sanders, *Jesus and Judaism*, London: SCM Press and Philadelphia: Fortress Press 1985.

**Grace:** But I'm not going to let you off the biblical hook so easily. There are three specific passages in the Synoptic Gospels which some interpret, and surely very reasonably, as implying a claim to deity on Jesus' part. One is the parable of the vineyard, in which the owner's son is killed (Mark 12. 2–6; Matt. 21.33–41; Luke 20. 9–18); a second is the Markan saying, 'But of that day or that hour no one knows, not even the angels in heaven, nor the son, but only the father' (Mark 13.32); and the third is the saying in Matthew, 'All things have been delivered to me by my father; and no one knows the son except the father, and no one knows the father except the son and anyone to whom the son chooses to reveal him' (Matt. 11.27/ Luke 10.22). Surely these show a clear consciousness on Jesus' part of his own divine sonship?

**John:** Well, as I said a moment ago, I turn to the New Testament experts to see how they interpret biblical passages. So let's turn again to James Dunn as a highly respected conservative scholar who wholeheartedly believes in Jesus' divinity. In his widely used *Christology in the Making* Dunn discusses the parable of the vineyard and says that 'the distinction between "servants" and "(beloved) son" in Mark 12. 2–6 provides no sure foundation [for the idea of Jesus' divine consciousness] since the contrast can be fully explained as part of the dramatic climax of the parable' (p. 28). And 'As for the other two sayings,' he says, 'it is precisely in Jesus' reference to himself as "the Son" that most scholars detect evidence of earliest Christians adding to or shaping an original saying of less christological weight' (p. 28). Thus the critical question is whether these sayings come in their present form from Jesus himself, or whether they've been touched up to express the belief of the Gospel writers; and this is something impossible definitively to determine. But to return to Dunn, having carefully examined not only these sayings but also all the other evidence in the Synoptic Gospels of Jesus' possible divine self-awareness, he speaks of 'the frustrating character of our evidence' and concludes that 'Just when our questioning reaches the "crunch" issue (Was Jesus conscious of being the divine Son of God?) we find that it is unable to give us a clear historical answer' (p. 29). And in the end I think the situation is that it's possible to fit the New Testament evidence into both a conservative and a liberal theological picture. We can't finally establish either from the texts, though we can use the texts to confirm them. I know that for some people this is difficult to accept, but nevertheless it seems to be the case.

## Two natures, divine and human?

**Grace:** Well without either accepting or rejecting that, let's move to the second of your three reasons to question the traditional incarnation doctrine.

**John:** Right. This is that the idea of Jesus' deity has never been able to be spelled out in an intelligible way. The official dogma asserts that Jesus was truly God and truly man, without attempting to say how this is possible. But there is an obvious problem about how an historical individual could have both all the essential divine attributes in virtue of which he is God and also all the essential human attributes in virtue of which he is a human being. How could Jesus be at the same time divinely omnipotent and humanly weak and vulnerable; divinely omniscient and humanly ignorant; the eternal, infinite, self-existent creator of the universe and a temporal, finite and dependent creature? Can such an idea be given any literal meaning?

**Grace:** Why not?

**John:** Well, the simplest possible literal conception of divine incarnation would be a divine mind in a human body. But this, and all the many ingenious variations on it, have had to be rejected as failing to do justice either to the deity or to the humanity of Jesus. Did God the Son then empty himself of his divine attributes in becoming a man? But is God without the attributes of God still God? And if Jesus had only those divine attributes that are not incompatible with being human, and only those human attributes that are not incompatible with being divine, could he be said to be either genuinely human or genuinely divine? There is a morass of difficulties here, and Christian orthodoxy has in the end only been able to say that the idea of the God-Man is a divine mystery which we cannot understand but must nevertheless revere. However, it's a mystery created by human beings through a process that we can trace historically, and in fact it's only a mystery in the sense of a form of words which has no clear literal meaning! It has a powerful metaphorical meaning, but has never yet been shown to have a viable literal meaning.[25]

**Grace:** And yet surely its power over the human heart depends upon its being believed to be literally true. So shouldn't we be content to accept it as a mystery, without raising the difficulties that you've highlighted?

## The deification of Jesus used to justify historical evils

**John:** That might be acceptable if the literally understood doctrine did not have literal implications which are so damaging to our relationship with the people of other faiths and which have also proved to be so well adapted to justify terrible human injustices and cruelties. This is the third of my problems with the traditional doctrine.

**Grace:** You've spoken about what you call the Christian superiority complex in relation to other faiths, but what do you mean by justifying terrible evils?

**John:** The absoluteness of the Christ figure has proved from the time of Constantine, the first Christian emperor, to the present day to be readily available to validate evils. There is no time now to describe this in detail. But European anti-Semitism justified itself for many centuries by the charge of deicide, which of course presupposes the deity of Jesus; and the secular anti-Semitism of the nineteenth and twentieth centuries, culminating in the holocaust of the 1940s, was only possible in a culture that had been prepared by centuries of Christian anti-Semitism, originally prompted by the anti-Semitic sayings in the Fourth Gospel.[26] For as Reinhold Bernhardt says, 'In the history of Christianity the theological condemnation of a religion has always been closely connected with the behaviour of Christians towards members of that religion'.[27] Again, Western colonialism, responsible for the

---

[25]For more about this, see John Hick, *The Metaphor of God Incarnate*, London: SCM Press 1993, and Louisville: Westminster/John Knox 1994, chs 5–7.

[26]For example, John 8.37; 8.44; 8.47.

[27]Reinhold Bernhardt, *Christianity Without Absolutes*, London: SCM Press 1994, p. x.

destructive exploitation of what we now call the third world, justified itself by the conviction that Christendom had a duty to impose true civilization and true religion – these being regarded as a unity – upon the inferior heathen peoples of the earth. This was the ideology which validated the political domination and economic exploitation of the third world. And yet again, patriarchialism, the assumption of a natural male superiority, was readily justified both by the maleness of the biblical image of God and the maleness of Jesus as God incarnate. In Mary Daly's famous phrase, 'When God is male, the male is God'.[28] This 'hidden agenda' has been evident in our own time in the arguments against the ordination of women in various branches of the Christian church, where we've been hearing arguments only a few stages further on from the mediaeval arguments about whether women have souls!

**Grace:**   I agree with you there. But is it fair to attribute all these evils to the church's incarnation doctrine?

**John:**   No, not as their direct cause. Their causes lie in human greed, selfishness, acquisitiveness, cruelty and prejudice. But the Incarnation doctrine has been readily available to justify those evils. In theory it would have been possible for Christians to believe that Jesus was God incarnate and yet not to have felt justified in persecuting and murdering Jews; not to have used the lordship of Christ to justify colonial annexations in India, Africa, North and South America, the Pacific islands and elsewhere; and not to have used Christianity to reinforce and validate male domination. If centuries of Christian influence had sufficiently modified our human greed, acquisitiveness and propensity to cruelty, the absoluteness of Christ could not have operated to justify ruthless aggression and persecution. But in fact human savagery has too often found Christian dogma tailored for its own self-justification. And this entire situation, consisting in the combination of an absolute claim together with a moral power-lessness which belies that claim, adds to the problematic character of the traditional dogma. In the light of this we should, surely, carefully re-examine it to see whether it really is an

---

[28]Mary Daly, *Beyond God the Father*, Boston: Beacon Press 1973, and London: The Women's Press 1986, p. 19.

essential part of Christianity. And I have been arguing that it not only lacks a secure historical grounding in the teaching of Jesus but also lacks any clear literal meaning.

Grace: I think I ought to mention at this point that some have gained the impression that you opt for an inspiration rather than a Chalcedonian christology simply because the latter has been used to justify the evils you have pointed to.[29] Is that correct?

John: No, as I think my philosophical critique of the Chalcedonian formula makes clear.[30]

Grace: At any rate, so far as the Incarnation doctrine itself is concerned, your conclusion is that we should simply abandon it?

## The metaphor/myth of God incarnate

John: No. I think we should recognize that it is not a literal truth, from which literal implications are to be drawn, but should affirm it instead as metaphorical truth.

Grace: This is something that came up in your discussion with Phil, but let's pursue it a little further. Just say again briefly what you mean by metaphorical or mythic truth.

John: A story is literally true if it corresponds with what is the case. So 'I ate an egg for breakfast today' is literally true if I ate an egg for breakfast today. A true myth, on the other hand, is a story which is not literally true but that nevertheless tends to evoke in the hearer an appropriate dispositional attitude to the story's referent, which in the case of myth always transcends the story itself. So the story that God (i.e. God the Son) came down from heaven to earth to be born as a human baby and to die on the cross to atone for the

---

[29]E.g., Paul J. Griffiths in *Christian Uniqueness Reconsidered*, op.cit. E.g. 'assent to the sentences expressive of an inspiration Christology makes possible the realization of theological and practical goals of which Hick approves on quite other grounds, and since these goals are less easily realized — and perhaps actively obstructed by — assent to the Chalcedonian formula, assent to the former is to be preferred to assent to the latter on that ground alone' (p. 159).

[30]See, e.g., my contributions to *The Myth of God Incarnate*, edited by myself (London: SCM Press, and Philadelphia: Westminster 1977); my contribution to *Religious Pluralism*, edited by Leroy S. Rouner (Notre Dame University Press 1984); and *The Metaphor of God Incarnate*, 1993, op.cit.

sins of the world is not literally true, because it cannot be given an acceptable literal meaning, but is on the other hand mythologically true in that it tends to evoke in us an appropriate attitude to the Divine, the Real, as the ultimate source of all salvific transformation, and thus as benign from our human point of view.

**Grace:**   But how do we know whether the response that a myth evokes is an *appropriate* response and is thus orienting us *rightly* to the Real?

**John:**   Well, in embracing the Christian myth we have entered the circle of religious faith, just as much as those who believe the story as literally true. Either way we have accepted it as the framework within which we respond to that which is ultimately real. In accepting it as myth or metaphor we are saying that it pictures our relationship to the ultimate in a particular set of human terms – and of course we have no other than human terms.

**Grace:**   I notice that you virtually equate myth and metaphor. But don't they have different meanings?

**John:**   Yes, but in my view a myth is an expanded metaphor. Both function to help us see something in a new light and so to react to it in a new way. But whereas a metaphor usually operates within a single sentence, a myth is a more or less developed story based on a metaphor. Thus we may think of God, metaphorically, as our heavenly Father, and we can develop this into the story of how the heavenly Father sent his Son down to earth to reconcile us to himself by dying for our sins; and so the story can grow – indeed has grown – into a whole theology.

**Grace:**   How does all this differ from the non-realist position of Feuerbach in the nineteenth century, or such writers as Santayana or Dewey or J. H. Randall, Jr in the United States, or in their very different ways R. B. Braithwaite or Don Cupitt in Britain? Surely the religious 'personae' and 'impersonae' can be appropriated as human constructions without having to postulate a transcendent Reality behind them? As one critic says, 'They may still be spiritually effective in the lives of different communities of faith even if there is no ultimate object of faith at all'.[31]

---

[31] Brian Hebblethwaite, 'John Hick and the Question of Truth in Religion' in Arvind Sharma (ed.), *God, Truth and Reality*, op.cit, p.130.

**John:** Yes, a naturalistic reduction of religion to a purely human construct is of course possible, and indeed represents the implicit or explicit view of many people today. But those who participate to any significant extent in one of the great historical streams of religious experience are, in my view, fully justified in trusting their religious experience as cognitive of a transcendent reality that is impinging upon them. But I have, as you know, argued at length elsewhere – as also have a number of others – for the rationality of forming beliefs on the basis of religious experience, and you won't want me to open up that large subject here.[32]

So the difference between a pluralistic religious understanding of religion, and the various non- and anti-realist understandings of it, is the difference between affirming and denying an ultimate transcendent Reality, which is the ground and source of everything, and which enters our human experience in the different ways made possible by the thought and practice of the different religions. In contrast to this, the non-realist thinkers deny that there is any such transcendent reality. They are non- or anti-realists, whereas the religious pluralist is a critical realist.

---

[32]John Hick, *Faith and Knowledge*, 1957, 2nd ed. London: Macmillan 1988, Part III, and *An Interpretation of Religion*, London: Macmillan, and New Haven: Yale University Press 1989, ch. 13; and William Alston, *Perceiving God*, Ithaca and London: Cornell University Press 1991.

# 5

# Salvation, Mission and Dialogue

## The Real as the Christian God in disguise

**Grace:** Let me turn now to some other criticisms. It's been said that in order to reject the old Christian exclusivism you have to appeal to the universal divine love which is incompatible with that exclusivism. But, some critics say, we only know of this universal divine love because it has been revealed to us in Jesus Christ. As one has put it, 'We only know that God is love and that there is salvation because of Christ'.[1] What do you say to this?

**John:** Well, of course, if, as a Christian, you restrict your attention within your own tradition, then Christ will be your only clue to the nature of the divine. But if you look more widely you see that it's not the case that, to quote another critic, 'The God of universal love at the centre cannot be spoken of or recognized without Jesus'.[2] The other major theistic faiths have their own independent grounds for this belief. The idea of the universal divine goodness/love/compassion is common to Judaism,[3] Islam[4]

---

[1] Chester Gillis, *A Question of Final Belief: John Hick's Pluralistic Theory of Salvation*, London: Macmillan and New York: St Martin's Press 1989, p. 170.

[2] Gavin D'Costa, *Theology and Religious Pluralism*, Oxford and New York: Blackwell 1986 p. 33.

[3] E.g., 'The Lord is gracious and merciful, slow to anger and abounding in steadfast love. The Lord is good to all, and His compassion is over all that He has made' (Psalm 148. 8–9).

[4] E.g., 'My mercy embraces all things' (Qur'an, 42.19); 'God is All-gentle to His servants, providing for whomsoever He will' (Qur'an, 42. 19).

theistic Hinduism,[5] Sikhism,[6] Jainism,[7] as well as Christianity. These are theistic forms of what I call the 'cosmic optimism' of the great post-axial traditions – their affirmation of the possibility for all human beings of a limitlessly better state grounded in the ultimate nature of reality. But this cosmic optimism is not confined to the theistic religions. In their own different ways Buddhism, advaitic Hinduism, and Taoism also share it. For they affirm the possibility of attaining a limitlessly better state, which they speak of as the attainment of Nirvana, or as the realization of oneness with the universal reality of Brahman, or as harmony with the eternal Tao.

**Grace:**   But when you say that all the great world traditions are forms of cosmic optimism, affirming a limitlessly good outcome of the project of human existence, aren't you forgetting the doctrine of eternal hell? This is hardly a good outcome for those who end up there – and according to St Augustine they are the majority of the human race.[8]

**John:**   No, you're right. There are elements within each tradition that work against its dominant character as good news, and the doctrine of eternal hell is probably the prime example. So I accept this correction, though I don't want to let it obscure the larger fact that each of the great traditions does present itself as good news for suffering humankind.

**Grace:**   OK. So returning to the main point, surely a Christian, at least, must affirm this cosmic optimism on the basis that Jesus, who taught God's fatherly love, was God incarnate, revealing the divine nature by his words and in his life and atoning death. And yet isn't this something that you deny?

**John:**   Yes, it is. Surely one doesn't have to believe that Jesus was the second person of a divine Trinity in order to accept his teaching

---

[5]E.g., 'In many forms of goodness, O Love, you show your face. Grant that these forms may penetrate within our hearts. Send elsewhere all malice!' (Atharva Veda, 9, 2. 24–5).

[6]E.g., 'The world is a garden, the Lord its gardener, cherishing all, none neglected' (Adi Granth, Majh Ashpadi, M.3, p. 118).

[7]E.g., 'Lord! You are the uninvoked saviour, motiveless compassionate being, a well-wisher even when unprayed, a friend even when unrelated' (Vitaragastava, 13.2).

[8]See, e.g., Augustine's *Enchiridion*, ch. 24, para. 97 .

about the love of God. If Buddhists can accept and live by Gautama's teachings in the *Sutras*, and Muslims the Prophet Muhammad's teachings in the *Hadith*, and Sikhs the teachings of their Gurus in the *Granth*, and so on, without believing that any of these great teachers was God incarnate, why cannot disciples of Jesus accept his parables of God's love without believing that he was himself God? Again, one does not have to believe that Jesus was God in order to see the divine goodness and love manifested (or in our Christian metaphor, incarnated) in his life – as in varying degrees in the lives of all true servants of God.

### Different salvations

**Grace:**   Well certainly that's consistent with your own christology, although of course very many Christians will regard it as fundamentally wrong. But let me move now to another criticism, taking up again the subject of salvation/liberation. You say that all the great post-axial religions – Hinduism, Judaism, Buddhism, Confucianism, Taoism, Christianity, Islam, Sikhism – exhibit a common soteriological structure. They are all, you say, concerned with salvation or, in your hybrid phrase, salvation/liberation – meaning that they seek to be contexts of human transformation from natural self-centredness to a new centring in the Real, the Ultimate, as differently conceived and experienced within them. But are you doing justice here to the profound diversity of the religions? Doesn't your idea of a common soteriological structure ignore, or rather conceal, the fact that they have different aims? Christian salvation is generally defined in Catholic thought as eventual union with the Blessed Trinity, and in Protestant thought as being forgiven and received into fellowship with God because of the atoning death of Christ – not of course that these two ideas exclude each other. But this aim is not shared by any of the other faiths. Each tradition has its own distinctive teaching about the ultimate aim of life and of the way we should live in view of that aim. And further, each holds that its own life-aim is the one most worthy of pursuit by all human beings.[9] And so one

---

[9]See, e.g. J. A. Dinoia, *The Diversity of Religions*, Washington, DC: Catholic University of America, 1992, and 'Pluralist Theology of Religions' in *Christian Uniqueness Reconsidered*, op.cit. See also John Milbank, 'The

writer claims that 'the soteriocentrism of [pluralistic theologies of
religion] seems bound to equalize or absorb the ineffaceably
particular soteriological programs of other religious communities'.[10] Don't you think there's something in this charge?

**John:**   From an exclusivist or an inclusivist point of view, yes;
from a pluralist point of view, no.

**Grace:**   How so?

**John:**   Well it's certainly true that the ideas of union with the
Holy Trinity, of nirvana, of Torah righteousness, of union with
Brahman, and so on, are each different and therefore unique.
That much is uncontroversial. But the question is whether
they're different forms of the more fundamental generic aim of
moving from a profoundly unsatisfactory state to a limitlessly
better state in right relationship to the ultimately Real. I think
they are. They diagnose the failure of ordinary 'unredeemed'
human life in different ways – as fallen sinfulness, or as the
blindness of *avidya*, or as a centring in the self-positing ego, and
so on. But these all refer to the same world-wide human condition with which we are so familiar. They each highlight a
different aspect of it and depict the limitlessly better state as its
reversal. But at whichever point our human condition is
grasped, it's changed as a whole in the transformation from
self-centredness to Reality-centredness.

**Grace:**   But surely the different traditions also teach different
moral and spiritual paths to attain their different aims.

**John:**   True. But these different paths are all forms of a gradual
transformation from self-centredness to a new centring in the
Real. In Christianity this is a conversion, in St Augustine's
language, from a heart curved in upon itself to a heart open and
responsive to the love of God; in Islam it's life lived in the security
and fulfilment of a complete submission to God; in theistic
Hinduism it's a fervent self-giving to Shiva, or to Vishnu

---

End of Dialogue' in *Christian Uniqueness Reconsidered*; Peter Fenner,
'Religions in the Balance', *Sophia*, Vol. 30, no. 1 (July 1991); and S. Mark
Heim, 'Salvations', *Modern Theology*, Vol. 10, no. 4 (October 1994) and
*Salvations*, Maryknoll, NY: Orbis 1995.

[10]J. A. Dinoia, *The Diversity of Religions*, op.cit, p. 43.

incarnate as Krishna, or to some other divine figure, all understood by educated Hindus as manifestations of the ultimate
reality of Brahman; in advaitic Hinduism it's a transcendence of
the finite ego into the infinite consciousness of Brahman; in
Theravada Buddhism it's the realization of the non-substantiality
of the self, bringing a loss of the ego point of view and a nirvanic
transformation of awareness; and in the Mahayana development
it's likewise a transcendence of the ego point of view, culminating
in the discovery that the process of *samsara* (ordinary human life
with all its pain and suffering), when experienced completely
unselfcentredly, is identical with *nirvana*.

**Grace:**   Yes, the idea of a radical change from self-centredness to
a new orientation centred in the Transcendent seems plausible in
these cases. But you didn't mention Judaism or, at the other end
of the world, Chinese religion; nor did you mention pre-axial and
extra-axial religion, such as African primal and native American
religion. And also what about the multitude of new religions that
are springing up all the time ?

## Other large and smaller and new religions

**John:**   Right. Let me say first that the salvific change doesn't
necessarily consist in a sudden conversion or illumination but
more usually in a gradual growing under the influence of a
nurturing tradition into a life centred in the sacred – though
sometimes this process does include a crucial 'threshold' experience of conversion or of enlightenment.

   That having been said, I believe that Judaism is clearly a salvific
path, as a form of life that moulds people into a right relationship
with God in preparation for the fulfilment of God's rule. There is
no time now to argue this in detail; but let me call in witness a
leading contemporary American Jewish thinker, Rabbi Irving
Greenberg, who says that 'The central paradigm of Jewish
religion is redemption',[11] meaning the full realization of the
image of God within us. And in China, Confucianism and Taoism

[11]Irving Greenberg, *The Jewish Way*, New York and London: Summit
Books 1988, p. 18.

are both ways to harmony with the ultimate order of the universe, Heaven (*T'ien*) or the Tao, in which the basic goodness of human nature is manifested. Confucianism – and it is generally better to speak of this rather than of Confucius himself, about whom we know very little – is a process of life leading from ego-concern to true sagehood. Its tendency has been 'to identify the transcendent with what is immanent, to acknowledge the presence of the way of Heaven in the way of man'.[12] But it's important to understand that, to quote Kang-nam Oh, 'Becoming a sage is not just a matter of becoming a morally respectable person, but rather a radical transformation of one's total being . . . a matter of ultimate transformation'.[13] This self-transformation, which is social rather than atomistically individual, is a never-ending, ongoing process of human maturation. Taoism also is concerned with moving from 'confusion and sorrow' to a limitlessly better state in harmony with the Tao, about which the *Tao Te Ching* says, 'If you don't realize the source, you stumble in confusion and sorrow. When you realize where you come from, you naturally become tolerant, disinterested, amused, kindhearted as a grand-mother, dignified as a king. Immersed in the wonder of the Tao, you can deal with whatever life brings you, and when death comes, you are ready'.[14]

**Grace:** And the pre-axial and extra-axial forms of religion, whose importance and value is being rediscovered today?

**John:** Yes, these are not, if I understand them rightly, salvific in the sense of seeking a radical human transformation, but are more concerned with keeping communal life on an even keel both in itself and in relation to the sacred. They are communal rather than individual responses to the Real. And in so far as they are effective, individual ego-transcendence is not called for because in traditional societies the autonomous ego has not become

---

[12]Julia Ching in Hans Küng and Julia Ching, *Christianity and Chinese Religions*, New York: Doubleday and London: SCM Press 1989, p. 89.

[13]Kang-nam Oh, 'Sagehood and Metanoia', *Journal of the American Academy of Religion*, Vol. 61, no. 2 (1994), p. 314.

[14]*The Tao Te Ching*, 16, trans. Stephen Mitchell, San Francisco: Harper & Row 1988.

detached from the unity of the social organism. You could say that primal religion is, ideally at least, religion before the 'fall' out of communal consciousness into individuality – a 'fall' which has been, negatively, the loss of truly integrated community, and positively, the achievement of individual autonomy – each of which has both its values and its limitations. That 'fall' was probably inevitable sooner or later. But there are immensely valuable aspects of primal religion that we in the individualistic industrialized world must try to recover – the sense of unity with nature, the awareness of the other animals as our cousins, a sense of responsibility towards the earth as the mother of all life.

**Grace:**   OK. And what about the multitude of smaller religions and new religions? For example, to go back no further than those originating in the nineteenth century, Mormonism, Christian Science, Baha'i, the Ahmadiyya movement, Tenrikyo, Spiritualism, Theosophy, Anthroposophy, Disciples of Christ, the Salvation Army . . . and twentieth-century religious movements such as Krishna Consciousness (ISKCON), Scientology, the Rastafarians, the People's Temple (the ill-fated Jim Jones movement), the Unification Church (the 'Moonies'), the Family of Love (formerly the Children of God), Soka Gakkai, Rissho Kosei Kai, Nichiren Shoshu, the Brahma Kumaris, the Kimbanguist church, the Lumpa church (founded by Alice Lenshina), Opus Dei, the Divine Light Mission, the Rajneeshees, the various 'New Age' movements, and other new or revived movements such as contemporary Voodoo, Satanism, Witchcraft, Wicker . . . and the list could go on.

**John:**   It could indeed. And of course we mustn't lump all these different movements together as though they were all of the same kind. Some are new variations within an existing world religion; others are movements formed around a charismatic leader, and some of these leaders have been either evil or insane whilst others have been morally and spiritually very impressive; some of the new religions are intrinsically local whilst others make a potentially universal appeal; and so on. Any judgment about them has to be based on a close examination of each particular movement, and all that one can say in general is that the same criterion must apply as in the case of the great world faiths: are they effective contexts of the salvific transformation of human beings from self-centredness to a new orientation centred in the Real as authentically known in a particular human way ? And the criterion of authenticity here can only be their observable moral and spiritual fruits in human life. I have confined myself in my own discussion to the centuries-old world religions because we have enough information about them to be able to discuss them against a reasonable background of common knowledge. I haven't myself made an equivalent study of any of the smaller or new movements that you listed – though I have encountered and been impressed by the Baha'i faith and by the Japanese religion of Tenrikyo, both originating in the nineteenth century. There is, however, one point that is worth making concerning many of the most recent, twentieth-century movements, at any rate in the West. This is that often they do not consist of a stable membership, beyond a small core, but are rather a revolving door with some people joining and others leaving all the time. Eileen Barker, who has intensively studied some of these movements, such as the 'Moonies' and the 'Hari Krishnas', says that 'there is a very high turnover rate, with far more people leaving the movements than staying in them for more than a limited period'.[15] It may be that these movements are able to meet a particular personal need at a particular time but lack the catholic comprehensiveness to provide a framework of meaning for large numbers of people throughout their lives. So perhaps many – but not all – of these movements have a part to play and a role to fulfil which is different from that of the great world faiths but which nevertheless has its own value.

## Two understandings of salvation and of Christianity

**Grace:**   OK. So going back now to the basic issue, there now seems to me to be an unbridgeable gap between two different conceptions of salvation or redemption. One can only be expressed in exclusively Christian terms, as union with the

---

[15]Eileen Barker, 'New lines in the supra-market' in Ian Hamnett (ed.), *Religious Pluralism and Unbelief*, op.cit., p. 34.

Blessed Trinity or as being forgiven by God because of the
atoning death of Christ (or as both); and the other is the view of
salvation as an actual human transformation, intended to begin
now, from natural self-centredness to a radically new orientation
centred in the Divine, the Transcendent, the Real. This gap is
recognized by Wolfhart Pannenberg when he writes, 'If salvation
is taken to refer to some [quoting you] "actual transformation of
human life from self-centredness to Reality-centredness", then
there is no reason to deny that such transformation occurs in
various cultures and in many forms of authentic religious
experience. But this is not [he says] the New Testament concept of
salvation. It is easy to check that there "salvation" was understood with reference to the eschatological judgment of God and
to participation in the communion of his kingdom'.[16]

**John:**    Yes, I think Pannenberg does point quite accurately to the
difference. And if you define salvation in exclusively Christian
terms, you are bound to end with an inclusivist (or an exclusivist)
theology of religions. Whereas if you define it as an actual human
change which is evident to much the same extent within all the
great faith traditions, then you will end with some form of
pluralist theology of religions.

**Grace:**    And I suppose the most basic criticism is that a pluralist
account of the world religions as different responses to the Real/
Ultimate/Divine is incompatible with the established self-understanding of Christianity as the one and only fully true religion.
For it denies the universal centrality of Christ as God incarnate.
As you've pointed out, if in Jesus we literally see God in person,
this revelation must in the nature of the case be definitive, final,
normative, incapable in this life of being equalled or exceeded.

**John:**    Yes, this is certainly the traditional Christian orthodoxy.
I was taught this in seminary, just as you no doubt were. My main
and much respected teacher there was the Presbyterian theologian H.H. Farmer, who in one of his books declared that 'in Jesus
Christ God came into history, took flesh and dwelt among us, in a
revelation of Himself, which is unique, final, completely adequ-

---

[16]Wolfhart Pannenberg in Gavin D'Costa (ed.), *Christian Uniqueness
Reconsidered*, op.cit., p. 101.

ate, wholly indispensable for man's salvation'.[17] The Pope would agree with this, as also does the World Council of Churches' basic formula, 'The Lord Jesus Christ as God and Saviour'. There can be no doubt that this is the traditional doctrine. But it is under challenge today precisely because it is so limited, only able to acknowledge the wider religious life of the human race by subordinating it to the Christian scheme of thought and thus distorting the true picture of our human situation. I pointed out in my lecture that it doesn't seem to be the case that Christians have in general been morally and spiritually superior to Jews in general, or Muslims in general, or Buddhists, Hindus, Sikhs, Taoists, Confucianists, Baha'is, or the peoples of the primal religions. And so there is a discrepancy between the official Christian self-understanding and the realities of human life, a contradiction between theological theory and observable fact. It is this that has led many of us to feel the need for revision.

Grace: Some will certainly deny that there is any such discrepancy, and will insist that Christians in general are indeed manifestly superior, morally and spiritually, to non-Christians in general. I'll leave it to others to argue that. But of course Christianity is not the only religion whose belief-structure implies its own unique superiority, is it ? After all, the Jews are uniquely God's chosen people; the Qur'an is God's final and unsurpassable revelation; the Vedas are *sanatana dharma*, the eternal truth; and according to the *Dhammapada*, the Buddhist dharma 'is the only Way. There is none other for the purity of vision'.[18] So are not the major traditions all in the same boat in this respect, each having aspects that a religious pluralist has to question?

John: Yes indeed. I suppose that traditional Christianity and traditional Islam have made the most explicit and emphatic claim to unique superiority; but all the others also do so, even if sometimes in less obtrusive ways. But there are also resources within each tradition with which it can, when its adherents so desire, go at least some way towards cancelling the old religious

---

[17] H. H. Farmer, *The Servant of the Word*, London: Nisbet 1941, p. 18.
[18] *The Dhammapada*, 20.2. trans. Narada Marathera, Colombo: Vajrarama 1972, p. 221.

chauvinism. We've already seen that Christianity can stress the idea of the universal Logos at work in all the great religions. In Judaism the very notion of the chosen people requires a complementary notion of God's relationship to non-Jews, and this is provided for some by the Noachite covenant – God's covenant with the human race as a whole – so that the rabbis could teach that 'the righteous of all nations have a share in the world to come'.[19] Again, the Qur'an not only accepts Jews and Christians as 'people of the Book' but affirms that God has given revelations both to 'many an apostle We have told you of before, and to many other apostles We have not told you of' (4. 164); and Islamic thought also includes the idea of the heavenly Book, *al-Qur'an al-takwini*, of which both the Qur'an revealed to the Prophet Muhammad and also the scriptures of other traditions are expressions. Hinduism is, in principle at least, readily able to accept other religions as paths to the Ultimate, and has even included their founders among the many incarnations of Vishnu. But whilst all these strategies move in the right direction they are all still forms of an inclusivism that extends the categories of one's own religion to include those outside its borders, but stops short of a full acceptance of them as equals.

Grace:   So none of the world religions can move beyond that point without reconstructing at least some part of its belief-system?

John:   Yes, I think that's the case. And there is a very liberating Buddhist teaching which I think could help. This is the view of religious doctrines, both its own and others, as 'skilful means' (*upaya*) enabling people to move in different ways towards the salvific transformation of enlightenment or awakening.

Grace:   I'm not familiar with this, so tell me more.

John:   Well we could start with the Buddha's parable of the man who is in danger where he is but sees safety on the other side of a stretch of water. Since there's no bridge or boat he takes branches and makes a small raft and paddles across to safety on the other side. And then, because the raft has been so useful he's tempted to lift it on to his shoulders and carry it with him. What he should

[19]Talmud, *Sanhedrin* 13.

do, however, now that the raft has served its purpose, is to go on, leaving it behind. Likewise, the Buddha said, the *dharma* (or in Christian terms, the gospel) is 'for carrying over, not for retaining . . . You, monks, by understanding the Parable of the Raft, should get rid even of (right) mental objects, all the more of wrong ones'.[20] Western readers of philosophy will be reminded of Wittgenstein's statement, 'My propositions are elucidatory in this sense: he who understands me finally recognizes them as senseless, when he has climbed out through them, on them, over them. (He must so to speak throw away the ladder, after he has climbed up on it.)'[21]

The basic thought is that religious teachings are not absolute and eternal truths but are human ideas that can help people to move at particular stages of their spiritual growth towards the goal of enlightenment, liberation, awakening or, in Christian terms, salvation. We each go through many stages of spiritual development – this is, incidentally, something that Hindu thought also stresses – and ideas and beliefs that are helpful, even vitally helpful, to us at one stage may cease to be at another. We know that children normally go through a series of stages to which different types of images and concepts are appropriate; and the same is true of the unfolding spiritual understanding of adults as we accumulate new life experience and new intellectual resources. We sometimes find that beliefs that were once full of meaning fade and die, whilst others that we once could hardly take seriously now come to life in our minds. You could even say, in a sense, that different visions of reality and different contexts of meaning become true for us at different points in our life journey.

**Grace:** And the Buddha actually applied this to his own teachings?

**John:** Yes, the *dharma* is only a means to attaining the experience of enlightenment or awakening. Its truths are human formulations about that which transcends human language and thought, though they can nevertheless be invaluable in leading people towards *nirvana*. This seems to me an extraordinarily

---

[20]*Majjhima Nikaya*, Book I, 134–5.
[21]Ludwig Wittgenstein, *Tractatus Logico-Philosophicus*, 6.54.

profound – indeed illuminated, liberated, awakened – self-understanding on the part of a religious tradition. And the same principle holds for Christianity and each of the other world faiths. They contain a rich variety of ideas, mental pictures, stories, concepts, doctrines and practices, some of which speak to one believer and others to another, and among which some may be more useful to a given believer at one point in her life, but different ones at another point. And the entire corpus of ideas, pictures, stories, doctrines, spiritual practices, social ethos and forms of life constituting a religious totality is only valuable as a means to an end – the end that we variously know as salvation, redemption, God-centredness, peace with God, enlightenment, awakening.

If each of the world religions could come to see both itself and the others in this way, they would allow people to grow within their own different faith-traditions, and would also be able to share spiritual resources across traditional borders.

## Christian mission

**Grace:**   This brings us very conveniently to something that we need to discuss, namely mission. What does all this mean for the Christian missionary movement?

**John:**   Well the word 'mission' has undergone a shift of meaning in recent decades, and so we need to be clear just what we're talking about. What most mainline Christian missionary societies are doing today is very different from what the missionary movement did for several centuries prior to the final breakup of the European empires after 1945. In that earlier period the great aim was to convert the world to Christianity. In the 1890s the Anglo-American student mission movement used the slogan 'the evangelization of the world in this generation', coined by the great missionary leader John R. Mott. By 1899 the British missionary societies alone had approximately 10,000 missionaries in the field – half as many missionaries as there were ordained Anglican clergy at home.[22] And the 'in this generation'

---

[22]A. N. Porter, 'Religion and Empire: British Expansion in the Long nineteeth Century, 1780–1914', Inaugural Lecture, King's College, London 1991, p. 3.

motto was used again to inspire the World Missionary Conference at Edinburgh in 1910.

Most of what we now call the third world was then ruled by the Christian first world. This was true of the entire Indian sub-continent, much of Africa, the Far East, South America, and the Middle East, where the Ottoman empire ended in 1919. Here the missionaries from Britain, France, Germany, Italy, Spain, Portugal, Sweden, Holland had more or less open access under the umbrella of a ruling foreign power. They made considerable progress in Africa and South America, although comparatively little in India, Asia, and the Far East. But in the more recent period the missionary societies have adapted to a new situation in which the former colonial territories are now independent states, within many of which there has been a powerful revival of Islamic, Hindu, Buddhist, or 'primal' consciousness. The result is that the Western missionaries are now either serving as priests and ministers within independent indigenous churches, or doing educational or medical work or providing agricultural and other expertise. The direct converting mission is now the province either of indigenous workers or of mainly well-funded US evangelical groups – the latter, however, often preying upon the existing Christian communities, trying to reconvert them to their own fundamentalist brand of Christianity, and thus dividing rather than enlarging the church. However, in so far as the missionaries of the mainline churches are acting in Christian love to share some of the technical resources of the industrialized West with the peoples of the third world, their work must surely be welcomed and applauded. But the older project, with which the word 'mission' is still indelibly associated in most people's minds, of converting the world to Christianity is from a pluralist point of view a complete mistake.

Grace:  I suppose that if the traditional converting mission does continue in any big way, it will probably emanate from such countries as Korea, where a strongly evangelical form of Christianity flourishes and where the new sources of industrial strength may prove to be. But, after all, if it were not for the early missionaries who brought Christianity to Europe, and thence to north America, you and I would not today be Christians, and nor would hundreds of millions of other people. In fact Christianity – if it had survived at all – would be no more than a Jewish messianic sect.

**John:**    Yes, true. But at this point we have to take a long historical view. The three great missionary religions have been Buddhism, Christianity, and Islam, each of which has spread far beyond its place of origin – indeed Buddhism and Christianity now have only a comparatively slight presence in their original homes. Each began in a place and time in which a major new religious impulse was needed and could succeed. Brahmanic India in the time of the Buddha, the religions of the Roman empire in the time of St Paul and the early church (the cults of Eleusis and Dionysus, Cybele and Attis, Isis and Osiris, Adonis and Mithras), and polytheistic Arabia in the time of the Prophet Muhammad, each left a spiritual vacuum for a new message of hope, giving fresh meaning to people's lives. Buddhism then moved after several centuries out of India into most of south east Asia; Christianity took over the declining Roman empire, inheriting the whole of Europe as its sphere, and later the colonial empires created by European conquests; and Islam exploded into the near East, Africa, Spain, and further east into India, Indonesia, southern Russia and China. And so in due course virtually the whole world was covered by these expanding movements, together with the remaining ethnic religions and innumerable smaller tribal religions. And since the global religious map thus became stabilized there has been little large scale conversion from one of the great world religions to another. For example, after a century and a half of unrestricted missionary activity in the Indian sub-continent, prior to independence in 1947, the Christian community amounts to only about two and a half per cent of the population. There have of course been, and no doubt will always be, individual conversions in all directions for individual reasons. But any proposal today to convert the whole world to Christianity, or for that matter to Islam or to any other faith, is today treason against the peace and diversity of the human family.

**Grace:**    But don't you think that the Christian gospel, by which we live, is a universal message which could be of benefit to anyone, wherever they may be? And so shouldn't it be made available to the whole world? Isn't there, then, a missionary obligation to spread it far and wide?

**John:** Yes, the gospel is a universal message which is for everyone to whose heart it speaks. And the message of Islam, and the Buddhist *dharma*, and the wisdom of the Indian sages embodied in what we call Hinduism, and again of Confuciansm and Taoism, are likewise universal and are for everyone to whose hearts they speak. All these different messages should be made universally available. The Bible, and the Qur'an, and the teachings of the Buddha, and the Upanishads and the Bhagavad Gita, and the Analects and the Tao Te Ching, and so on, should all be available in multiple translations throughout the world. In this sense each faith does have its own legitimate world-wide mission to conduct.

**Grace:** So there is a place for missionary movements after all.

**John:** Yes, though not in the sense of an attempt to convert those who are committed to another of the great world religions. But when there is a free flow of religious influences it is always possible that someone who hears the Christian or the Muslim or the Buddhist etc. message will find that, in the Quaker phrase, it speaks to their condition and they come to embrace what is to them a new faith. We probably all know former Muslims who have become Christians and former Christians who have become Muslims, former Buddhists and Hindus who have become Christians, former Christians who have become Buddhists or Hindus, Jews who have become Christians or Buddhists, Christians who have become Jews, and so on. But these are individual conversions for individual reasons and they are numerically insignificant in comparison with the massive transmission of each tradition from generation to generation within its own families and communities.

**Grace:** So you would like us to disband the converting missions but to encourage the translation and distribution of the sacred scriptures and secondary writings of every tradition, and accurate knowledge about them, as well as the peaceful dialogue of people of different faiths.

**John:** Yes, that's about it.

## Dialogue

**Grace:**   So let's turn to that peaceful dialogue between religions. I know that you are in favour of this because you've been actively involved in it for a number of years.

**John:**   Yes, during the last twenty-five years, with Hindus in India and in the West, with Sikhs in the Punjab, with Buddhists in Sri Lanka, Japan, and the United States, with Jews and Muslims in Britain and the USA, and also with Jews in Israel; and I was a founding member of both the Buddhist-Christian Theological Encounter group and the International Scholars' Jewish-Christian-Muslim dialogue group. Partly out of all this, but also independently of it, I have Jewish, Muslim, Hindu and Buddhist friends. There are plenty of people with far more experience of this kind than me; but I have found that getting to know people, both ordinary people and a few extraordinary individuals, of other faiths is a much more valuable way of coming to understand their tradition than the reading of many books. Of course one must read the many books, but often they only give you the official picture of a religion, which needs to be filled out, and sometimes corrected, by personal contacts. So yes, I am in favour of inter-faith dialogue.

**Grace:**   Well as you know, my concern is with criticisms that have been levelled against religious pluralism. And the main point that I hear concerning dialogue is that the conflicting beliefs of the dialogue-partners should be retained and be frankly argued out rather than in any way reduced or politely concealed. As one critic says, 'Dialogue between those who assume in a rather woolly fashion that in all fundamentals they are in agreement and that their differences are secondary and unimportant is unlikely to be other than tedious and unproductive.'[23] What do you say to this?

**John:**   Well, there are several different kinds of inter-religious dialogue. There is the kind that this critic evidently thinks desirable, in which a Christian, for example, tries to persuade a

---

[23]Duncan Forrester, 'Professor Hick and the Universe of Faiths', *Scottish Journal of Theology*, Vol. 29, no. 1 (February 1976), p. 71. See also, for example, Julius Lipner on 'reduction dialogue' in 'Truth-Claims and Inter-Religious Dialogue', *Religious Studies*, Vol. 12, no. 2 (June 1976), p. 227.

Muslim that the Prophet Muhammad's experience of hearing the words of the Qur'an came from his own unconscious mind, rather than being dictated by Gabriel on behalf of God, or in which a Muslim tries to persuade a Christian that Jesus was not God incarnate – and so on through all the innumerable differences of belief among the world's religions. But this kind of polemical dialogue is usually fruitless except in producing alienation and enmity. I'm sure that the official belief-system of each tradition is capable of desirable development and modification at many points; but this can only properly be done from within those traditions and by their own thinkers. I, as a Christian theologian, have a responsibility to try to contribute to the continuous re-forming of Christian doctrine, particularly in the light of our new awareness of the other world faiths. But it is not for me to presume to tell my Muslim or Jewish or Hindu or Buddhist colleagues how to try to develop their own traditions in response to the same new awareness.

**Grace:** So in inter-faith dialogue you never argue or criticize?

**John:** Oh, I do. In situations of mutual trust and respect I have raised critical questions both about some of the beliefs and some of the practices of other traditions; and I have also heard critical questions raised about some Christian beliefs and practices. And it can sometimes be very salutory to be told how others see us. But in the end change has to come from within a religious tradition.

**Grace:** And is change in fact taking place?

**John:** Yes, to a certain extent, though the big institutionally organized movements are at present moving in the other direction, leading back towards fundamentalism. But just as there are today a large number of Christian theologians whose input is bringing about a gradual change in the outlook of thoughtful Christians, so also there are Jewish, Muslim, Hindu, and Buddhist thinkers – though probably in smaller numbers – doing analogous work within their own traditions. And this is often prompted by a different kind of inter-faith dialogue than the polemical.

**Grace:** This other kind being . . . ?

**John:** Well for example in the Buddhist-Christian dialogues that I've been part of for a number of years until very recently, involving about twenty Christian theologians, mostly from the United

States, and about twenty Buddhist scholars, mostly from Japan and the USA, representing the Zen and Tibetan traditions, we have studied together basic Buddhist and Christian ideas and texts. On the Christian side we have been fascinated to learn about such very alien-to-us concepts as *anatta* ('no self'), *sunyata* ('emptiness'), and *upaya* ('skilful means'). In these meetings, and in other individual meetings outside them, some of us have also been interested to see the effects of the practice of *zazen* and of Tibetan forms of meditation in a noticeable degree of detachment from self-concern and a flowering of serenity and kindness. This encounter with Buddhism is affecting the way in which a number of leading American theologians are doing their work. None has become a Buddhist, but I think all have been impressed by Buddhist insights and values and by their embodiment in a number of Buddhists. It's not for me to say how our Buddhist colleagues have been affected by their encounters with Christianity. But there can be no doubt that intellectually serious and personally friendly sharing and comparing of ideas, histories, and experiences, even between people of traditions which are theoretically as different as Christianity and Buddhism – one being theistic and the other non-theistic – can be extremely valuable. There can be a mutual influencing which may even lead at some future time to a degree of convergence in which the two traditions can see themselves as different responses to the same ultimate mystery. And the same with the other great traditions.

**Grace:**    You've been talking about organized dialogue between religious professionals. But what about more ordinary everyday encounters?

**John:**    Yes, these are at least as important, and in fact probably more so. In several countries people of different faiths have long been accustomed to live together, often as neighbours and friends. In these situations a kind of implicit religious pluralism prevails, each in practice regarding the other as legitimately following their own strangely different inherited tradition.

**Grace:**    But on the other hand there are plenty of situations in which religious differences operate to validate and intensify political conflicts – the Iran-Iraq war, the Bosnian-Serbian war, Hindu-Muslim communal conflicts in India, the Republican-

Unionist conflict in Northern Ireland, the Israeli-Palestinian conflict and in many other areas where religion has been turned from a blessing into a curse. To take just one case, is it not noticeable that in the Israeli-Palestinian dispute it has been the most religious people on both sides – in the sense of those with the most absolute religious beliefs – who have constituted the biggest obstacle to a peaceful solution?

**John:** Yes indeed. And this can happen because the absolutist aspect of each faith motivates young men to be willing to kill and be killed for a sacred cause. The absoluteness of the justification – God's will, or holy church, or a revered tradition – can have power to validate anything. But if this absoluteness were dismantled by the realization that one's own religion is one among several valid human responses to the Divine, religion could become a healing instead of a divisive force in the world.

**Grace:** OK. We must come now to a final question. You claim, as you've just said, that the great world faiths are different human responses to the same ultimate reality. It would seem to follow, then, that in so far as they come to accept this they should unite, so that one day there will be a single global religion. Is this your view?

**John:** No, it isn't. Just as the continuing variety of human cultures is of great value, so also is the continuing variety of forms of religion. What is to be hoped for in the future, I would think, is that the different traditions, while continuing to be distinctively different, will each gradually winnow out the aspect which entails its own unique superiority, and increasingly influence one another in interfaith dialogue, with some degree of mutual transformation in which each enriches and is enriched by the others. Eventually, we may hope, the relationship between the religions will be rather like that between most of the main sections of Christianity today. So far at least as the mainline churches are concerned, though admittedly with occasional lapses, we have each come to recogize the others as different but legitimate forms of Christianity. I do not, for example, as one formed by Presbyterianism,[24] have to think that Catholics,

----

[24]I was ordained in the Presbyterian Church of England, which has subsequently united with the Congregational Union of England and Wales to form the United Reformed Church.

Baptists, Lutherans, Congregationalists, Episcopalians, Quakers, and so on, ought all to become Presbyterians, though I can and do think that some of the other churches could learn something from the Presbyterian tradition and that Presbyterians can learn something from those other traditions. And I think it is likewise becoming true that we do not as Christians have to think that Buddhists and Muslims and Jews and Hindus ought to become Christians, although we may well think that they can all learn something from Christianity and that Christianity can in turn learn something from each of them. But the only sense in which there may one day, even in the remotely foreseeable future, be a single world religion is that the continuing traditions may come to see one another as different forms of response to the same transcendent Reality.

**Grace:**    All right. I don't know how far I agree with that; but nevertheless the Real be with you!

**John:**    And with you also.

# 6

# A Christianity That Sees Itself as One True Religion Among Others

## Christianity's changing character

The broad pluralistic vision of the great world religions as different but independently valid human responses to the ultimate reality that we call God is today widespread among Christians, and particularly among those who know people of other faiths as neighbours or fellow-citizens. They show this more often in their practical dealings with those neighbours than in explicitly formulated beliefs. For many people it has become an assumption of daily life that our Jewish or Muslim or Hindu or Sikh or Buddhist friends and acquaintances are as fully entitled in the sight of God to live by their own religious traditions as we are to live by ours. In thus regarding them as having their own authentic form of faith, rather than pitying them as lost souls, we are operating with an implicitly pluralistic theology. We feel no obligation to try to convert them to Christianity, but have on the contrary come to see them as related to God, or the ultimately Real, in their own different way.

However, it is a function of philosophy and theology to make explicit and consistent what our experience has led us to accept implicitly. And when we do this here we find that religious pluralism challenges some of our traditional dogmas. It does not require that any of the basic Christian ideas be abandoned, but that they be understood afresh in non-traditional ways. These new ways are jointly indicated by the findings of modern biblical scholarship and by our experience of the moral and spiritual fruits of the other world faiths. New Testament scholarship has shown that the historical Jesus did not claim to be God incarnate and that what we know as the doctrines of the Incarnation, Trinity, and Atonement have escalated into theoretical constructions going far beyond the original experience to which they are related. They have then become official and defining dogmas which by implication single out the life and death of Jesus as the only locus of salvation, and Christianity as the only religion to have been founded by God in person. And yet – and here is the problem – this implied religious superiority is not confirmed by the actual life of the church or of Christian individuals or cultures. It is this joint impact of modern New Testament scholarship and of a perceived lack of superior fruits in human life that has led to a changing conception of Christianity and its place in the world.

But can there be a form of Christianity which reveres Jesus as its supreme teacher and inspirer but does not regard him as literally God incarnate; which seeks to nurture men and women from self-centredness towards a new centring in God, thus promoting not only individual but also social and national and international unselfishness; and that sees itself as one major spiritual path among others, developing friendly and co-operative relations with those others?

The question is really two questions, one theological and the other ecclesiastical.

Theologically, we have to ask whether this would still be Christianity? Is not a Christian one who believes at least the central Christian doctrines; and does not this proposed revision abandon those central beliefs? The first step is to assert the principle that Christian belief is, quite simply, what Christians generally believe, and to note that this has varied enormously over the centuries. But is it possible for there to be the kind of major development, or 'paradigm shift', that religious pluralism invites? When we look back historically at the ever changing shape of Christian belief the answer has to be Yes. For although the great Christian words and symbols – God, Christ, Trinity, the Virgin Mary, the Cross, Church, Body and Blood, Heaven and Hell, and so on – have remained constant through the centuries, their meaning has varied to a startling extent as between different times and places.

I can illustrate this from a cross-section of Christianity in a typical part of mediaeval Europe. Dennis Nineham has recently investigated what Christianity meant to ordinary believers in northern France around the end of the first millennium. When we compare their religious outlook a thousand years ago with ours in the mainline churches today, we find that, apart from the institutional continuity of the church, there is hardly anything in common beyond our use of the same great symbols. For us today God is, above all, infinite love. For them God was a remote, arbitrary, terrifying power. The contrast could hardly be greater. Whereas we see ourselves as the children of a heavenly Father, they saw themselves as serfs of an all-powerful Lord whose honour was offended by their disobedience, so that most men and women were destined to the eternal torments of hell. To quote Nineham:

> In an age which, as we have seen, had little understanding of secondary causes, the evils that befell society were assumed to be punishment from God; he must indeed be angry with his people, it was felt, if he visited so much suffering upon them. At the personal level also, the deaths and illnesses of individuals were interpreted as divine punishment for what they had done, even if in many cases no one could be sure what this had been. God was believed capable of bringing about the slaughter of countless enemy troops – mostly conscripts at that – to ensure the victory of an army which had won his favour; and it must be remembered that orthodox doctrine had no doubt or qualms about his intention to damn the great majority of the world's population, including all babies who died unbaptized. Small wonder if such a heavenly lord seemed quite as arbitrary and high-handed as any earthly lord.[1]

For, as Nineham says, 'To most people, as we have seen, God

---

[1]Dennis Nineham, *Christianity Mediaeval and Modern*, London: SCM Press 1993, p. 48.

himself appeared as a formidable, remote and inscrutible lord, intensely concerned about his honour, and unwilling to show favour until it had been fully satisfied. He was implacable to his foes, a God who had no hesitation in visiting eternal torture on the great majority of his human creatures, including many who had had no opportunity of knowing about him, and all who had died unbaptized in infancy. Not only baptism but complete acceptance of the Christian creed, particularly at the moment of death, was an absolute condition of enjoying his favour.'[2]

Today we think of Jesus primarily in his humanity, fully sharing the pains and sorrows of human life, and often as on the side of the poor and oppressed and thus the validator of our demand for justice and peace on earth. But in the mediaeval world 'Jesus during his earthly life was believed to have been God the Son in person, in the full panoply of his divine attributes, whose assumption of humanity had involved no loss of omniscience and omnipotence and who was overseeing the universe at the very moment when he was sucking his mother's milk or uttering his parables in Galilee'.[3] He was pictured as 'the *pantocrator*, the ruler of all, portrayed with crown, throne, sun, moon, the alpha and omega, symbols of universal power, and worshipped by hosts of angels and the adoring elders of the Old Testament'.[4] He did not really signify divine love come down to our human level, as in the minds of so many Christians today. There was, apart from the important exception of the mystics, little sense of a living personal relationship with Christ or God:

In whatever connexion one sought to approach the divine, one worked through ecclesiastically-provided means, which tended, at least, to be thought of as effective *ex opere operato*, and in most cases required the intermediacy of the clergy. In such a transactional atmosphere, personal relationship with God was apt to fade into the background. Just as the king was too remote a figure for immediate contact, and had to be ap-

---

[2]Ibid., p. 231.
[3]Ibid., p. 234–5.
[4]Ibid., p. 47.

proached through one of his courtiers, so for most people God was an infinitely remote and formidable figure, only to be approached through friends at court, the angels, or, more commonly, the saints. It was only with the saints that any personal relationship, not to say intimacy, was to be expected; only from them that any real warmth or loving-kindness was to be experienced in the religious sphere. Even Jesus was not the object of devotion he was to become later. It was undoubtedly the saints who were the real object of a great deal of early mediaeval piety, and, as we have seen, they were taken in practice for virtually independent powers who answered prayer and worked wonders in their own right. In the matter of forgiveness and acceptance with God, one's only real hope lay in them and their willingness to plead on one's behalf.[5]

All this is far removed from the Christianity of the typical Catholic or Orthodox or Lutheran or Reformed or Anglican or Methodist or Pentecostal congregation today. And if we ask how it is that the great Christian words and symbols can have been used to express such widely different meanings, the answer obviously lies in changes that have taken place at the human end of the divine-human relationship.

This is illustrated again by the way in which successive understandings of the significance of the cross of Christ have reflected the socio-political conditions of the society in which they arose. In the first and longest period, covering almost a thousand years, the cross was mainly understood in terms suggested by the idea of ransom, deriving from Jesus' saying that 'the son of man came not to be served but to serve, and to give his life as a ransom for many' (Mark 10.45). In the world of Jesus' own time a large part of the population were enslaved, either as prisoners of war or as citizens of a defeated city or country, or as children of such, and to be ransomed from slavery was a powerful metaphor for a new life released from the domination of sin. But the church made its almost invariable mistake of taking the metaphor literally, asking the inevitable question: To whom was

---

[5]Ibid., p. 232.

the ransom paid? 'To whom gave he his life "a ransom for many"? It cannot have been to God. Was it not then to the evil one? For he held us until the ransom for us, even the soul of Christ, was paid to him.'[6] This was for many centuries the way in which the meaning of the cross was understood, not only by simple people but also by seminally influential theologians such as St Augustine.

However, in the eleventh century St Anselm, freeing himself from the existing paradigm, asked how the devil could have valid legal rights over against the infinite Creator?[7] This led him to propose instead a 'satisfaction' theory, reflecting the current state of European society in which the rule of law expressed the will and power of a feudal lord. To break his law was to impugn his rights and insult his honour, so that adequate satisfaction had to be made, either by the punishment of the wrongdoer or by some acceptable alternative; and Jesus' death was seen as a full and final satisfaction offered to God for the sins of the world.

By the time of the Reformation, however, five centuries later, law had come to be seen differently, no longer as stemming from a ruler's will but now as an objective requirement to which even the ruler is subject. God, it was said, was a just as well as a loving God, and as such he could not waive the immutable moral law that required the proper punishment for sin. So God the Son, in his infinite love, bore in our place the inexorable penalty for the sins of the world. But this idea is also open to obvious criticism. How could it be just to punish the innocent instead of the guilty? And, more fundamentally, do not all these ideas, whether of a ransom to be paid, or a satisfaction to be given, or a punishment to be borne, exclude any idea of genuine forgiveness of the truly penitent? For instead of free forgiveness there is merely the registering of the fact that the debt has been paid in full!

And so the death of Jesus has become for many Christians today the manifestation of a self-giving love which is an earthly reflection of the divine love, rather than an atoning transaction to

---

[6] Origen, quoted by L. W. Grensted, *A Short History of the Doctrine of the Atonement*, Manchester University Press 1962, p. 38.

[7] St Anselm, *Cur Deus Homo*, Book I, ch. 7.

enable God to forgive sinners. But this represents a transformation of Christian understanding that would, until within about the last century, have seemed utterly heretical and, at one time, deserving the direst penalties.

I have already referred (p. 85) to the way in which, during the last hundred years, the Catholic 'outside the church there is no salvation' dogma has been gradually emptied of meaning in order to avoid its horrific implications. But the most recent major transformation within Christian belief as a whole has been a result of the 'warfare of science with theology'[8] caused by the irresistable explanatory power of Darwin's theory, first published in 1859, of the evolution of the species by natural selection, which was incompatible with the biblical belief in the creation of the different species as they now are and of humanity as a special creation set apart from animal life; and at the same time by the discovery of the geologists that the age of the earth has to be measured in millions of years, thus shattering the biblical chronology according to which it was created only some 6,000 years ago. Running parallel with these scientific discoveries modern 'biblical criticism' began to study the scriptures as historians examine other ancient literature. Beginning with the Old Testament this type of analysis questioned the Mosaic authorship of the Pentateuch; distinguished different and incompatible strands of tradition, with different conceptions of God, in the creation stories and elsewhere; and uncovered within the biblical narratives vast political distortions of ancient history – thus undermining the accepted belief in the verbal inspiration of the Bible. Then New Testament scholarship dismantled the natural assumption that the Gospels were four eye-witness accounts of Jesus' life, and worked out their approximate dates, beginning some forty years after Jesus' death, showing how Matthew and Luke are dependent on Mark, and how John's Gospel depicts a largely different Christ from the earlier 'synoptics', noting numerous contradictions between the four

---

[8]This was the title of the book by A. D. White, President of Cornell University, *A History of the Warfare of Science with Theology in Christendom* (1896), 2 vols, New York: Dover Publications 1960.

narratives, and also beginning to see Jesus as a genuinely human figure in the context of the Judaism of his time. All this made it possible to regard the New Testament as a collection of human writings expressing a particular faith response to God and thus as the Word of God in a metaphorical sense rather than as literally the words of God.

Today we take for granted the shape of Christian belief that has resulted from the impacts of modern science and modern biblical scholarship. But the change from the belief-system of our great-great-grandfathers amounts to nothing less than an intellectual revolution which they would then have regarded with horror as signifying the end of Christianity! We see a similar phenomenon today in the fear that the acceptance of Christianity as one valid human response to the Divine among others would mean its demise! As in the case of previous theological transformations, it would be *either* its death, *or* its rebirth in a new stage of human awareness, this time the stage of global consciousness.

Theologically, then, the changed Christian self-understanding called for by the recognition of our place within the wider human picture, is feasible and is indeed unavoidable if there is to be a credible Christian faith for the twenty-first century.

But is this possible ecclesiastically? Is it practically possible, given the existing institutionalized forms of Christianity, so largely controlled by Popes, Patriarchs, Cardinals, Archbishops, Bishops, General Assemblies and annual Conferences?

The fact that church leaders are, generally speaking, averse to change is not in itself theologically significant. This has been the case ever since Christianity was adopted in the fourth century as the established religion of the Roman empire. Within the church there are a variety of different vocations, and it is the recognized role of ecclesiastical rulers to conserve the inheritance of the past rather than to engage in new explorations. This is an important and necessary role, worthy of full respect. But it is also necessary that there be others who explore new paths of thought in the ever-changing human situation. And when (as we see in the nineteenth century science/religion debates) after the publication of many books and journal articles, causing long discussion at many levels and gradually producing incremental shifts in outlook, a new consensus eventually emerges, the official church leadership will then endorse it, and it will be orthodoxy! This has happened all through history; and so long as Christianity is a living and developing stream of religious life, it will continue to happen.

We must, however, remember that theological change is never a clean break with the past. On the contrary, discarded doctrines normally continue within the churches' liturgies, so that we still today speak in church of Adam and Eve and their Fall as though these were real individuals and a real event in the distant past; of Jesus' death on the cross as a ransom or satisfaction or punishment on our behalf; and of darkness over pagan lands which must be saved from perdition by the light of the gospel. But, more importantly, there is a vast area of Christendom, both in the traditionally Christian West and in its former foreign mission fields, which has never assimilated the theological changes so largely accepted within the main-line Western churches, consisting in the wide range of fundamentalist and evangelical forms of discipleship to Jesus.

Numerically, probably the large majority of Christians, as also of the adherents of each of the other world religions, are conservative or traditional believers. There is, however, a difference between the unreflective conservatism of the majority who practice their faith with little or no concern for theological issues, and the articulate conservatism of the fundamentalist and evangelical Christianity which began in the early 1900s in conscious reaction against a developing liberal Christianity, and which has today become such a large and powerful movement with its own right-wing political as well as religious agenda. At present the divide between fundamentalist/evangelical and liberal Christianity runs through the different denominations rather than between them. There are Christians of both types – or rather both families of types – within almost all the churches. There are thus two minds, understanding the world differently, within the same ecclesiastical body.

Looking to the future, one possibility is that the body will also split into two, so that there will then be visibly two Christianities. If this happens, one will be predominantly fundamentalist, but also including under its wing some evangelical and ultra-conservative elements, and the other liberal and probably increasingly diverse – with each seeing the other as a religious disaster. However, this would be a highly regrettable development. On the one hand, it would leave millions of Christians in an intellectual twilight zone, subject to the influence of sometimes dangerous fundamentalist extremists. For it is noticeable that in so many areas of bitter confrontation today – for example, in the Israeli-Palestinian conflict, in the Catholic-Protestant conflict in Northern Ireland, and so on – it is the fundamentalists on both sides who do most to intensify and prolong the conflicts. It should, however, be added that there are also many within the fundamentalist/evangelical wing of Christianity to whom the criticism that their faith tends to intensify political conflicts does not apply. But nevertheless it is undeniable that absolutism in religion, preaching the unique superiority of one's own tradition over against others, continues to motivate young men to be willing to kill and to be killed for what they regard as a sacred cause. And on the other hand a split between the two Christianities would leave other millions with a freedom to experiment but in danger of losing contact with their ancestors in the faith – who include great saints and mystics and thinkers as well as others who have used religion as a form of social control and as a validator of human oppression and exploitation. As regards the development of Christian belief, it is greatly preferable for the two Christianities to continue, even if with constant friction, to co-exist within the same ecclesiastical frameworks; for there is then the possibility of dialogue and mutual influence and of the more convincing ideas gradually prevailing.

## A view from the year 2056

Let us now make a giant leap of the imagination and consider what the state of Christianity may be in two generations time within the more liberal or progressive wing of Christianity if the pluralistic vision continues to gain acceptance within it. The other, fundamentalist/evangelical wing will, I anticipate, continue to be powerful, and may even have separated itself into a distinct church structure, or structures. But here I consider the changes that may come about within a Christianity that has come to see itself, no longer as the one and only true faith, but as one among several.

Speaking in the present tense, as from the year 2056 of the Common Era, the predicted slow demise of religion under the onslaught of secularizing modernity and 'post-modernity' has not occurred. It still seems as though the human race is innately religious, with an ineradicable tendency to think of the natural in the light of the supranatural. The attempt to educate whole populations out of this, in Russia and China, has failed; and new forms of religion, including secular forms, continue to arise in bewildering profusion. The largest world religions, numerically, are now Islam and Christianity, each including (at least nominally) about one and a quarter billion men and women. The rapid growth of Islam, which overtook Christianity early this century, peaked some twenty-five years ago as the population explosion in the third world came to an end. There has also been a large expansion of the influence of Buddhism in the West; and also of new syncretistic forms of spirituality.

The Christian churches are still divided into Roman Catholicism, Eastern Orthodoxy, and the churches stemming from the Reformation of the sixteenth century, but the relations between them are much closer and more friendly, and various mergers have taken place among the Reformed movements. The Catholic church began to ordain women to the priesthood early in the present century and within a generation a number of women rose into the episcopacy. The great reforming pope, John XXIV, has made a number of them Cardinals, and although they are not a majority in the College of Cardinals it is nevertheless widely expected that the next pope will be a woman.

The life of the churches continues essentially as in the past, even though the prevailing theology, and therefore some of the language, has been changing during the last fifty years. Services of worship are still, in varying degrees, occasions when people congregate to open their hearts and minds to the overarching divine reality, and are renewed in their basic trust in the source of all life. They are enabled by the stories, poetry, metaphor, imagery, and dramatic ritual of an ancient and rich tradition to rejoice together in the goodness of the creation and to comfort and support one another in life's hardships, restrictions, failures and tragedies. And in doing so they find one another, and encourage one another to work for fairness and peace in their own society and in the wider world. The central messages of liberation theology, feminist and womanist theology, and ecological theology, have been assimilated and the mainline churches have been increasingly dedicated to working for social justice, gender equality, and a sustainable human life-style which preserves the fragile balance of the global environment. Christianity is 'greener' and more humane and politically responsible than in the past.

Theologically, divine incarnation in human life is now seen as taking place whenever and wherever God's will is freely done. So understood, 'incarnation' does not signify having two complete natures, one divine and the other human, but is a metaphorical way of speaking about openness and obedient response to God – so that whenever a man or a woman freely does the divine will, in that action God becomes incarnate on earth. Jesus' life is seen as an outstanding occasion of divine incarnation. The idea of the Trinity no longer involves three mysteriously inter-related centres of divine consciousness and will, but is a symbol for the three-fold character of our human awareness of God – as the creative source of all life, as the transforming salvific power, and as the divine spirit living within us.

In those sections of the universal church in which the pluralistic vision has become established, worship is explicitly directed to God, rather than to Jesus, or to the Virgin Mary or the saints. This has been the result of a continuous process of liturgical revision, increasingly finding its central inspiration in the Lord's Prayer. Revisionists emphasized that in this prayer we are taught to address God directly as our heavenly Father, and not through any mediator, and to ask for forgiveness, expecting to receive it – the only condition (but it is a big condition!) being that we forgive one another. There is no suggestion that God's acceptance of us is conditional upon Jesus' death as an atoning sacrifice. Indeed there is no reference in this prayer, taught by our lord himself, to the ideas of incarnation, trinity or atonement that the church was later to develop.

Within both common and private worship, prayers of adoration, thanksgiving, confession, and intercession have continued essentially unchanged from the twentieth century, except that God's goodness and mercy are not now sought 'for Jesus' sake' but on the ground of the eternal divine nature.

The traditional sacraments have continued to be practised as a vital aspect of church life. The eucharist is seen as the central symbolic act, linking us in historical memory with Jesus and his first disciples and in solidarity with one another and with our predecessors in the faith through the ages. Baptism continues as the dedication of a child to God and as his or her reception (as also in the case of an adult) into the church. Marriage is thought of by some as a sacrament, and by others as the solemnizing and blessing of a wedding. Funerals continue as always. It is here that the division between, on the one hand, non-realist and, on the other hand realist (or, more accurately, critical realist) understandings of religion comes to a head. As was already the case fifty years ago, those clergy who have opted for non-realism regard the idea of our present life as part of a much larger existence within which the human project eventually comes to fulfilment, as a fiction, whilst other clergy and lay people take it very seriously – some drawing support for belief in continued life after death from developments in parapsychology, and an increasing number showing sympathy for various forms of reincarnation belief.

The 'Apostles'' Creed is still generally used, not, however, as a literal expression of contemporary belief but as a symbol of the continuity of the church through the ages – as indeed it probably was by many people fifty years ago. Whilst numerous new hymns have been written, and new music produced, during the last two generations, many older ones continue, the poetic power of their imagery being treasured and enjoyed long after it has ceased to be understood literally.

Congregations continue to follow their own differing traditions of worship, whether of a solemn liturgy with beautiful words and music and the impressive symbolism of processions and robes and bells and incense and icons, or of very informal worship using popular language and music and drama, perhaps hand clapping and dancing in the aisles; and everything in between these extremes. Healing services, with the laying on of hands, are more common now that the psychosomatic aspect of illness and the interactive psychic network of which we are all part have become more widely accepted. In other parts of the church such practices as speaking with tongues, the 'raising of holy hands', being 'slain in the spirit', and so on, continue among those who find them helpful.

Relations with the other world religions are now generally good, being based on a formal acceptance of their independent validity, although this acceptance is still compromised by powerful fundamentalist Christian groups seeking to convert Jews, Muslim, Buddhists, Hindus, Sikhs, and others. The World Council of Churches is still trying to include both Christianities within itself and is therefore still unable officially even to recognize that there is salvation outside Christianity. Inter-faith co-operation is now widespread in work for social justice and fairness, and internationally in work for world peace and the protection of mother earth.

The missionary activity of the church is not now directed to people of other faiths but to the post-Christian majority of the nominally Christian countries. It has thus involved a change of direction in the work of many of the more constructive theologians. Instead of being concerned with the elaboration and reinterpretation of traditional Christian doctrines – a work that continues but is no longer a central concern, – they are developing different approaches, in a strongly science-oriented and secular-minded age, to belief in a transcendent divine Reality which gives a framework of meaning to human life. For they have gradually realized that outside the churches there is a great religious concern and hunger that can never again be satisfied by the older version of Christianity as a self-enclosed faith claiming exclusive truth. However, it now seems that an overarching spirituality that takes Christian as well as other forms strikes a chord in many open and searching minds. In this context, whilst the traditional Christian doctrines have ceased to be of interest to most people, there is a widespread concern with the basic issues of the nature of the universe and our place in it, with the meaning of human life, with the nature of good and evil, with our relationship to other forms of life, with the question of death and of a possible afterlife. An undogmatic Christianity, centred on the person and teachings of Jesus, is being heard again, alongside the teachings of Buddhism and of Hinduism and Islam and other traditions.

## Spirituality in a pluralistic age

When we have come to see the other great religious traditions as different but (so far as we can tell) equally valid human responses to the ultimate reality that is the ground and source of everything and the condition of our highest good, we have no reason to restrict ourselves to the spiritual resources of our own tradition. This is our home ground; but just as a citizen of the United States, or Britain, or France, or Japan, or any other country, can become a better informed and more open-minded citizen, through travel abroad, learning other languages, reading other literatures, contact with other cultures, so also in the realm of the spirit. As Christians we can usefully explore some of the methods of meditation developed within the Buddhist and Hindu traditions, where meditation is far more widely, and often more expertly, practised than among ourselves. And when we feed our minds and hearts by reading the scriptures and the writings of great saints, we do not need to restrict ourselves to the Bible and to Christian writers.

The only effective way of making this point is to give some examples of what we may encounter when we travel abroad in the spirit; and so what follows is a brief anthology drawn from a range of accessible non-Christian writings. The sources are given in the footnotes, but the passages are meant to be read through and appreciated for their own sakes as expressions of different human awarenesses of the Transcendent. I shall not draw here from the Hebrew scriptures because they are already familiar to us as our Old Testament. But something from Jewish prayer and from the sayings of the rabbis in the Talmud can begin this little collection:

At Judgment Day everyone will have to give an account for every good thing which he might have enjoyed but did not enjoy.[9]

> A certain heathen came to [Rabbi Hillel] and said to him:
> Convert me provided that you can teach me the entire Torah
>> while I stand on one foot . . .
> Hillel . . . said to him:
> What is hateful to you, do not do to your neighbour:
>> This is the entire Torah;
>>> the rest is commentary;
>>> go and learn it.[10]

O servant, where dost thou seek Me ?
Lo! I am beside thee.
I am neither in temple nor in mosque:
  I am neither in Kaaba nor in Kailash:
Neither am I in rites and ceremonies,
  nor in Yoga and renunciation.
If thou art a true seeker, thou shalt at once see me:
  thou shalt meet Me in a moment of time.
Kabir says, 'O Sadhu! God is the breath of all breath'.

I laugh when I hear that the fish in the water is thirsty:
You do not see that the Real is in your home,
  and you wander from forest to forest listlessly!
Here is the truth! Go where you will, to Benares or to Mathura;
  if you do not find your soul, the world is unreal to you.[11]

---

[9]Jerusalem Kiddushin 66d, quoted in Arthur Hertzberg, *Judaism*, New York: Simon & Schuster 1991, p. 244.

[10]Babylonian Talmud, Shabbat 31a. Hillel, who died about 10 CE, was a great Talmudic teacher.

[11]*Songs of Kabir*, I and XLIII, trans. by Rabindranath Tagore, New York: Weiser 1977, pp. 45 and 91. Kabir lived in India in the fifteenth century and was revered by both Hindus and Muslims.

I am the flavour in water,
    the radiance in the sun and moon,
The basic, sacred word in sacred texts,
    the sound in the highest element,
And, Arjuna, I am
    what makes men *men*.

I am the scent of promise in the earth
    and the burning strength in the fire,
The life in all creatures
    and the ascetic fire in holy men.

Son of Pṛthā, know me as the
    perennial seed in all that lives.
I am the understanding of those who understand,
    the majesty of the majestic.

I am the strength of the strong,
    free from lust and passion,
And I am, Strongest of Bharatas,
    the right desire in living beings.[12]

There is but one God. He is all that is.
He is the Creator of all things and He is all-pervasive.
He is without fear and without enmity.
He is timeless, unborn and self-existent.
He is the Enlightener
And can be realized by grace of Himself alone.
He was in the beginning; He was in all ages.
The True One is, was, O Nanak, and shall forever be.[13]

---

[12]*The Bhagavadgita*, ch. VII, 8–11, trans. by Kees Bolle, Berkeley: University of California Press 1979, p. 87. The *Gita* is probably the most widely read Hindu scripture.

[13]The Japji, part of the morning prayer, first recited by Guru Nanak, the founder of the Sikh tradition in the fifteenth century, trans. by Harbans Singh, *Guru Nanak*, Bombay, London, and New York: Asia Publishing Co. 1969, pp. 96–7.

The One God is the Father of all,
We are all his Children.

The One God is the cause of all causes,
Knowledge, wisdom, discrimination are His gifts to us;
He is not far, He is not near, He is with us all.
Saith Nanak: Praise the Lord with abiding love.[14]

If one speaks or acts with wicked mind, because of that, suffering follows even as the wheel follows the hoof of the draught-ox . . . If one speaks or acts with a pure mind, because of that happiness follows one even as one's shadow that never leaves.

Hatreds never cease through hatred in this world; through love alone they cease. This is an eternal law.

All tremble at the rod. All fear death. Comparing others with oneself, one should neither strike nor cause to strike.[15]

May all be happy and safe!
May all beings gain inner joy —
All living beings whatever . . .
Seen or unseen.
Dwelling afar or near,
Born or yet unborn —
May all beings gain inner joy.
May no beings deceive another,
Nor in any way scorn another,
Nor, in anger or ill-will,
Desire another's sorrow.
As a mother cares for her son,
Her only son, all her days,
So towards all things living

---

[14]From the *Adi Granth*, the Sikh Bible, Nanak V, Sorath, p. 611, and Gaudi, p. 235, quoted by Trilochan Singh, 'Theological Concepts of Sikhism' in Darshan Singh Maini (ed.), *Sikhism*, Patiala: Punjabi University Press 1969, p. 44.

[15]*The Dhammapada*, a widely used collection of sayings of the Buddha, trans. by Narada Mahathera, Colombo: Vajirama 1972, pp. 1, 5, 8, 123.

A man's mind should be all-embracing.
Friendliness for the whole world,
All-embracing, he should raise his mind,
Above, below, and across,
Unhindered, free from hate and ill-will.[16]

People go to their temples
To greet Me;
How simple and ignorant are my children
Who think I live in isolation.

Why don't they come and greet Me
In the procession of life, where I always live,
In the farms, the factories and the market
Where I encourage those
Who earn their bread by the sweat of their brow?

Why don't they come and greet Me
In the cottages of the poor
And find Me blessing the poor and the needy
And wiping the tears of the widows and orphans?

Why don't they come and greet Me
By the road-side
And find Me blessing the beggar asking for bread?
Why don't they come and greet Me
Among those who are trampled upon
By those proud of power and riches,
And see Me beholding their suffering and pouring out
    compassion.

And why don't they come and greet Me
Among women sunk in sin and shame
Where I sit by them to bless and uplift?

I am sure

---

[16]*Sutta Nipata*, 143ff. William de Bary (ed.), *The Buddhist Tradition*, New York: Vintage Books 1972, pp. 37–8. The *Suttas* of the Pali canon constitute the basic scriptures of Buddhism.

they can never miss Me
If they try to meet Me
In the sweat and struggle of life
And in the tears and tragedies of the poor. [17]

There is a thing inherent and natural,
Which existed before heaven and earth.
Motionless and fathomless,
It stands alone and never changes;
It pervades everywhere and never becomes exhausted.
It may be regarded as the Mother of the Universe.
I do not know its name.
If I am forced to give it a name,
I call it Tao, and I name it as supreme. [18]

I died as mineral and became a plant,
I died as plant and rose to animal,
I died as animal and I was Man.
Why should I fear? When was I less by dying?
Yet once more I shall die as Man, to soar
With angels blest; but even from angelhood
I must pass on: all except God doth perish. [19]

God is the Light of the heavens and the earth;
    the likeness of His Light is as a niche
    wherein is a lamp –
        the lamp is a glass,
    the glass as it were a glittering star –
        kindled from a Blessed Tree,

---

[17]Kushdeva Singh, *In Dedication*, Patiala: Guru Nanak Mission 1974, pp. 31–2. Kushdeva Singh, who died in 1985, was a Sikh mystic and activist who created a range of caring institutions in the city of Patiala in the Punjab, India.
    [18]*Tao Te Ching*, ch. 25, trans. by Ch'u Ta-Kao, London: Mandala Books 1982, p. 44.
    [19]*Rumi: Poet and Mystic*, LXI, trans. by R. A. Nicholson, London: Mandala Books 1978, p. 103. Jalaluldin Rumi, who died in 1273 CE, was one of the great Sufi writers of Islam.

an olive that is neither of the East nor of the West
whose oil wellnigh would shine, even if no fire touched it;
　　Light upon Light;
　　God guides to His Light whom He will.[20]

God rebuked Moses, saying, 'O thou who hast seen the
　　rising of the moon from thy bosom,
Thou whom I have illumined with My Light! I am God,
　　I fell sick, thou camest not.'
Moses said, 'O transcendent One, Thou art clear of defect,
　　What mystery is this? Explain, O Lord!'
God said unto him again, 'Wherefore didst not thou
　　kindly ask after Me when I was sick?'
He answered, 'O Lord, Thou never ailest. My understanding
　　is lost: unfold the meaning of these words.'
God said, 'Yea; a favourite and chosen slave of Mine fell sick.
　　I am he. Consider well:
His infirmity is My infirmity, his sickness is My sickness.'[21]

A sickness is not cured by saying the word 'medicine'. You must
take the medicine. Liberation does not come by merely saying
the word 'Brahman'. Brahman must be actually experienced.[22]

Return love for great hatred.
Otherwise, when a great hatred is reconciled, some of it
　　will surely remain.
How can this end in goodness?
Therefore the sage holds to the left half of an agreement
　　but does not exact what the other holder ought to do.
The virtuous resort to agreement;

---

[20]*Qur'an*, from surah 24, trans. by Arthur J. Arberry, *The Koran
Interpreted*, London and New York: Oxford University Press 1964,
pp. 354–5.

[21]*Rumi: Poet and Mystic*, op. cit., XXIX, p. 65.

[22]Shankara, *Crest-Jewel of Discrimination*, trans. by Swami
Prabhavananda and Christopher Isherwood, Los Angeles: Vedanta Press
1978, p. 41. Shankara (eighth century CE) was one of the greatest and most
influential of Hindu thinkers.

The virtueless resort to exaction.
The Tao of heaven shows no partiality;
It abides always with good men.[23]

> Those who love and believe in God without knowing God are
> the ones who best know God.[24]

Grandfather Great Spirit,
All over the world the faces of living ones are alike.
With tenderness they have come up out of the ground.
. . . Give us the strength to understand
and the eyes to see.
Teach us to walk the soft Earth as relatives of all that live.[25]

He who accepts gladly the sufferings of this world brings
salvation to the world.[26]

'Our sages say that men should praise and thank God for
suffering just as much as for wellbeing, and receive it with the
same joy. Will you tell us how we are to understand this, Rabbi?'
The Rabbi replied, 'Go the House of Study. There you will find
Zusya smoking his pipe. He will give you the explanation.' They
went and put their question to Rabbi Zusya. He laughed. 'You
certainly have not come to the right man! Better go to someone
else rather than me, for I have never experienced suffering.' But
they knew that, from the day he was born to this day, Rabbi
Zusya's life had been a web of need and anguish. Then they knew
what it was to accept suffering with love.[27]

---

[23]*Tao Te Ching*, op. cit., ch. 79.

[24]Kitaro Nishida, *An Inquiry into the Good*, trans. by Masao Abe and
Christopher Ives, New Haven and London: Yale University Press 1990,
p. 176. Nishida, who died in 1945, was a founder of the Kyoto school of Zen
Buddhist philosophy.

[25]From the Sioux of North America. Elizabeth Roberts and Elias Amidon,
(eds), *Earth Prayers*, San Francisco: HarperSanFrancisco 1991, p. 184.

[26]Talmud, *Ta'an*, 8a.

[27]Martin Buber, *Tales of the Hasidim*, I, New York: Pantheon, 1947,
pp. 217–8.

Only His extreme nearness to you
  is what veils God from you.

He made the Hereafter an abode
  to reward His believing servants
only because this world cannot contain
  what He wishes to bestow upon them
and because He deemed their worth too high
  to reward them in a world without permanence.[28]

Death is not extinguishing the light, but putting out the light because the dawn has come.[29]

These samples are a reminder of the enormous wealth of varied riches that await us in the spiritual writings of humankind around the world and through the centuries. The pluralist point of view prompts us to take advantage of them, and I believe that everyone who does so will find that there is nothing to fear, but on the contrary great benefit to be gained, from this wider vision. There are a number of excellent anthologies that make such material readily available.[30]

---

[28]Kwaja Abdullah Ansari, *The Book of Wisdom*, trans. by Wheeler Thackston, New York: Paulist Press 1978, and London: SPCK 1979, pp. 65 and 88. A Sufi Muslim.

[29]From Rabindranath Tagore, who died in 1941. Tagore was a Bengali poet and thinker who did much to introduce Hindu thought to the West.

[30] Perhaps the best at present is Philip Novak, (ed.), *The World's Wisdom: Sacred Texts of the World's Religions*, San Francisco: HarperSanFrancisco 1994. Other excellent ones are Bede Griffiths (ed.), *Universal Wisdom: A Journey Through the Sacred Scriptures of the World*, London: HarperCollins and San Francisco: HarperSanFrancisco 1994, and Ninian Smart and Richard Hecht, (eds), *Sacred Texts of the World: A Universal Anthology*, London: Macmillan, 1992. A larger volume is Andrew Wilson, (ed.), *World Scripture: A Comparative Anthology of Sacred Texts*, New York: Paragon House 1991. An older publication is Robert Ballou, (ed.), *The Pocket World Bible*, London: Routledge & Kegan Paul 1948, and published in the USA as *Living Bible*, New York: Viking Press 1952.

# Appendix I

# Some Thanks and Explanations

This book is an expanded version of the Auburn Lectures delivered in April 1994 at Union Theological Seminary, New York, as the first in a new series instituted to celebrate the 175th anniversary of the founding of Auburn Seminary. I am grateful for the honour of this invitation, and to President Barbara G. Wheeler and Dean Robert E. Reber of Auburn, and President Holland Lee Hendrix of Union, and to Professor Vincent L. Wimbush and Professor Linda Perkins, for their splendid hospitality to my wife and me during our very enjoyable stay at Union. Each lecture was followed by responses from distinguished theologians – Kwok Pui-Lan of the Episcopal Divinity School, Cambridge, Massachusetts; Eugene B. Borowitz of Hebrew Union College, New York; Walter Philip Wink of Auburn Seminary; and Ivone Gebara of Auburn Seminary, to each of whom I am grateful for their contributions.

I was asked to respond in the lectures to criticisms of religious pluralism. The request presupposes a distinction between religious plurality, as the fact that there are a number of religions, and religious pluralism as a family of theories about the relationship between the religions. Pluralistic theories stand in contrast to exclusivist theories, according to which one's own religion is exclusively the location of salvation/liberation/enlightenment, and to inclusivist theories according to which one's own religion embraces people of other religions within its own exclusively authentic salvation or liberation or enlightenment. In distinction from these, pluralistic theories acknowledge the other great world religions as independently authentic spheres of salvation/liberation/enlightenment. A range of pluralistic points of view have been offered by recent and contemporary writers. These do not by any means all agree with one another, either about how to think through a pluralistic outlook, or even about whether it is appropriate to try to develop a comprehensive theory at all. And so there have been and will continue to be strong arguments among some of those who hold a broadly pluralistic view – and some of these arguments surface in this book.

My own particular version of religious pluralism holds that the great world religions constitute very different but so far as we can tell more or less equally valid ways of conceiving, experiencing, and responding in life to the ultimate reality with which religion is concerned; and it is criticisms of this particular version that I was asked to respond to. My response to these criticisms, however, is not always an attempted rebuttal. I have over the years learned a good deal from careful criticisms, and am grateful for them and have at several points developed my understanding further in the light of them. I might add that several of the leading critics are personal friends, some of whom are also former students or colleagues; though this does not prevent us from disagreeing profoundly.

I have not turned the original project into a different and much larger one by discussing other forms of religious pluralism, or into a still larger one by discussing the alternative responses to religious diversity in the exclusivist and inclusivist theologies of religion.

Even this limited task, however, is complicated by the sheer mass of literature that has already accumulated around these issues. I am only one of a number of theologians and philosophers who have independently developed a broadly pluralist point of view. But a glance at Appendix II will show the size of the critical discussion of my own formulation – and the list does not include an equally large number of discussions in books, varying in length from a page or two to a chapter. I am probably the only person who has had occasion to read all of this material; and there may well be yet other items of which I am not at the moment aware, so that very probably no one has actually read the whole lot! And when we add the equally numerous criticisms directed to other religious pluralists I think it can confidently be said that no one has ever read the entire corpus. I might add that a complete bibliography of the entire subject, parallel to Barry Whitney's recent excellent one on Theodicy,[1] although a big task, would be a very valuable resource to have.

How to go about responding to the critics? I have already (see Appendix II) replied in print to a few of the critical articles, either in the same or a subsequent issue of the journal in which they appeared.[2] But it would have been neither useful nor interesting to reply one by one to all of them now. For often the same points recur, and it seems much more sensible to address the main criticisms themselves than to respond to each different formulation of them. Further, a detailed reply to an article or chapter only makes sense when the reader or the audience has recently read the piece under discussion. And so I have responded to issues rather than to authors, though with brief quotations to anchor the discussion in the literature. The drawback of this procedure is of course that critics who read this book will not find here a direct response to their own article or chapter as such, though they will I hope find each of their main concerns discussed at some point.

The dialogue form seems particularly suitable for such an exercise, and so after the opening lecture (now chapter 1) in which my own version of religious pluralism is put forward, the discussion proceeds by dialogue. Here I am in conversation with Phil and Grace, dealing with philosophical and theological issues respectively – though of course these cannot always be clearly separated. Their parts were taken in the Auburn lectures themselves by Jace Garrett Weaver and Annie Ruth Powell, both then PhD candidates at Union Seminary. My thanks again to both of them. I have retained the relatively informal language that seemed appropriate before a live audience and that may, I hope, now also make the material more easily readable.

I am grateful to Mark Heim, Werner Ustorf, and Franklin J. Woo for specialized advice.

---

[1]Barry L. Whitney, *Theodicy: An Annotated Bibliography on the Problem of Evil*, 1960–1990, New York and London: Garland Publishing Inc. 1993.

[2]In addition to the replies listed in the Appendix, responding to particular articles, there is 'Straightening the Record: Some Responses to Critics', *Modern Theology*, Vol. 6, no. 2 (January 1990).

# APPENDIX II

My version of the pluralistic hypothesis is presented in *An Interpretation of Religion* (London: Macmillan, and New Haven: Yale University Press 1989); *Problems of Religious Pluralism* (London: Macmillan, and New York: St Martin's Press 1985); *God and the Universe of Faiths* (London: Macmillan, and New York: St Martin's Press 1973, and Oxford: One World Publications 1993); *God Has Many Names* (London: Macmillan 1980, and Louisville: Westminster/John Knox 1982); *The Metaphor of God Incarnate* (London: SCM Press 1993, and Louisville: Westminster/John Knox 1994); and in the following edited works: *The Myth of God Incarnate* (London: SCM Press, and Louisville: Westminster/John Knox 1977); with Hasan Askari, *The Experience of Religious Diversity* (Aldershot, England and Brookfield, Vermont: Gower Publishing Company 1985); and with Paul Knitter, *The Myth of Christian Uniqueness* (Maryknoll, NY: Orbis, and London: SCM Press 1987).

## Critical Discussions

### Books

Gavin D'Costa, *John Hick's Theology of Religions: A Critical Examination*, New York and London: University Press of America 1987.

Chester Gillis, *A Question of Final Belief: John Hick's Pluralistic Theory of Salvation*, London: Macmillan and New York: St Martin's Press 1989.

Gregory H. Carruthers, *The Uniqueness of Jesus Christ in the Theocentric Model of the Christian Theology of World Religions: An Elaboration and Evaluation of the Position of John Hick*, New York and London: University Press of America, 1990.

Gavin D'Costa (ed.), *Christian Uniqueness Reconsidered*, Maryknoll, New York: Orbis 1990.

Harold Hewitt (ed.), *Problems in the Philosophy of Religion: Critical Studies of the Work of John Hick*, London: Macmillan and New York: St Martin's Press 1991.

Arvind Sharma (ed.), *God, Truth and Reality: Essays in Honour of John Hick*, London: Macmillan and New York: St Martin's Press 1993.

Chris Sinkinson, *John Hick: Introduction and Assessment*, Leicester: UCCF/RTSF, 1995.

Hiromasa Mase and Hisakazu Inagaki (eds), *Explorations in Religious Pluralism: John Hick Studies*, Tokyo: Teimeido 1995.

## Journal articles

M. Warner, 'The Uniqueness of Christ', *Modern Churchman*, Vol. 18 (Winter 1974).

Duncan Forrester, 'Professor Hick and the Universe of Faiths', *Scottish Journal of Theology*, Vol. 29, no. 1 (February 1976).

Julius Lipner, 'Truth-claims and Inter-religious Dialogue', *Religious Studies*, Vol. 12, no. 2 (June 1976).

Stanley Russell, 'The Finality of Christ and Other Religions', *Epworth Review*, Vol. 4, no. 1 (February 1977).

Julius Lipner, 'Does Copernicus Help?', *Religious Studies*, Vol. 13, no. 2 (June 1977).

Peter Byrne, 'John Hick's Philosophy of World Religions', *Scottish Journal of Theology*, Vol. 35, no. 4 (August 1982). [Reply: 'The Philosophy of World Religions', Vol. 37, no. 2 (June 1984).]

Philip Almond, 'John Hick's Copernican Theology', *Theology*, Vol. 86, no. 709 (January 1983). [Reply: 'The Theology of Pluralism', Vol. 86, no. 713 (September 1983).]

Ulrich Berner, 'Das Christusverstandnis als Gegenstand universalgeschichtlicher Betrachtungen', *Saeculum: Jahrbuch fur Universalgeschichte* (1983).

Paul Griffiths and Delmas Lewis, 'On Grading Religions, Seeking Truth, and Being Nice to People – a Reply to Professor Hick', *Religious Studies*, Vol. 19, no. 1 (March 1983). [Reply: 'On Conflicting Religious Truth- Claims', Vol. 19, no. 4 (December 1983).]

Kenneth Surin, 'Revelation, Salvation, the Uniqueness of Christ and Other Religions', *Religious Studies*, Vol. 19, no. 3 (September 1983).

L. Philip Barnes, 'Towards a Theology of World Religions', *Churchman*, Vol. 97 (1983).

Craig Kubias, 'John Hick's Epistemology: A Viable Basis for World Theology?', *Church Divinity* (1983).

Dewi Arwel Hughes, 'Christianity and Other Religions: Review of Some Recent Discussions', *Themelios*, Vol. 9, no. 2 (January 1984).

Gavin D'Costa, 'John Hick's Copernican Revolution: Ten Years After',

*New Blackfriars*, Vol. 65, nos 769/770 (July/August 1984).

Gavin D'Costa, 'Elephants, Ropes and a Christian Theology of Religions', *Theology*, Vol. 88, no. 724 (July 1985).

William Forgie, 'Hyper-Kantianism in Recent Discussions of Mystical Experience', *Religious Studies*, Vol. 21, no. 2 (June 1985).

Harold Netland, 'Professor Hick and Religious Pluralism', *Religious Studies*, Vol. 22, no. 2 (June 1986).

Roger Corliss, 'Redemption and the Divine Realities: A Study of Hick and an Alternative', *Religious Studies*, Vol. 22, no. 2 (June 1986).

Anselm Min, 'Christology and the Theology of Religions: John Hick and Karl Rahner', *Louvain Studies*, Vol. 11, no. 1 (Spring 1986).

Mary Ann Stenger, 'The Problem of Cross-cultural Criteria of Religious Truth', *Modern Theology*, Vol. 3, no. 4 (July 1987).

Gerard Loughlin, 'Noumenon and Phenomena', *Religious Studies*, Vol. 23, no. 4, (December 1987).

Chester Gillis, 'John Hick's Christology', *Bijdragen, tijdschrift voor filosofie en theologie*, Vol. 49 (1988).

David Basinger, 'Hick's Religious Pluralism and "Reformed Epistemology": A Middle Ground', *Faith and Philosophy*, Vol. 5, no. 4 (October 1988).

Robert McKim, 'Could God Have More than One Nature?', *Faith and Philosophy*, Vol. 5, no. 4 (October 1988).

Paul J. Griffiths, 'An Apology for Apologetics', *Faith and Philosophy*, Vol. 5, no. 4 (October 1988).

Schubert Ogden, 'Problems in the Case for a Pluralistic Theology of Religions', *The Journal of Religion*, Vol. 68 (October 1988).

Hiromasa Mase, 'John Hick's Religious Pluralism', *Philosophy* (Keio University), Vol. no. 88 (June 1989).

Kenneth Surin, 'Towards a "Materialist" Critique of 'Religious Pluralism': A Polemical Examination of the Discourse of John Hick and Wilfred Cantwell Smith', *The Thomist*, Vol. 53, no. 4 (October 1989).

Gerard Loughlin, 'Prefacing Pluralism: John Hick and the Mastery of Religion', *Modern Theology*, Vol. 7, no. 1 (October 1990). [Reply: 'Response to Gerard Loughlin', Vol. 7, no. 1 (October 1990).]

Gavin D'Costa, '"Extra ecclesiam nulla salus" Revisited', in Ian Hamnett (ed.), *Religious Pluralism and Unbelief*, London and New York: Routledge 1990.

Kenneth Surin, 'A Certain "Politics of Speech": "Religious Pluralism" in the Age of McDonald's Hamburger', *Modern Theology*, Vol. 7, no. 1 (October 1990).

L. Philip Barnes, 'Relativism, Ineffability, and the Appeal to Experience: a Reply to the Myth Makers', *Modern Theology*, Vol. 7, no. 1 (October 1990).

Keith Ward, 'Truth and the Diversity of Religions', *Religious Studies*, Vol. 26, no. 1 (March 1990).

Hendrik Vroom, 'Do All Religions Worship the Same God?', *Religious Studies*, Vol. 26, no. 1 (March 1990).

Gavin D'Costa, 'Taking Other Religions Seriously: Some Ironies in the Current Debate on a Christian Theology of Religions', *The Thomist*, Vol. 54, no. 3 (July 1990).

Sumner B. Twiss, 'The Philosophy of Religious Pluralism: A Critical Appraisal of Hick and his Critics', *The Journal of Religion*, Vol. 70, no. 4 (October 1990).

Timothy R. Stinnett, 'John Hick's Pluralistic Theory of Reigion', *The Journal of Religion*, Vol. 70, no. 4 (October 1990).

Rebecca Pentz, 'Hick and Saints: Is Saint-Production a Valid Test?', *Faith and Philosophy*, Vol. 8, no. 1 (January 1991).

Peter Byrne, 'A Religious Theory of Religion', *Religious Studies*, Vol. 27, no. 1 (March 1991).

B.J. Verkamp, 'Hick's Interpretation of Religious Pluralism', *International Journal for Philosophy of Religion*, Vol. 30, no. 2 (October 1991).

Peter Fenner, 'Religions in the Balance', *Sophia*, Vol. 30, no. 1 (July 1991).

Paul Badham, 'John Hick and the Human Response to Transcendent Reality', *Dialogue and Alliance*, Vol. 5, no. 2 (Summer 1991).

John V. Apczynski, 'John Hick's Theocentrism: Revolutionary or Implicitly Exclusivist?', *Modern Theology*, Vol. 8, no. 1 (January 1992).

Eric Springsted, 'Conditions of Dialogue: John Hick and Simone Weil', *The Journal of Religion*, Vol. 72, no. 1 (January 1992).

Philip Barnes, 'Continuing Development in John Hick's Theology', *Studies in Religion*, Vol. 24, no. 4 (1992).

Paul Badham, 'John Hick's Global Understanding of Religion', Tokyo Honganji, Lecture Series II–4, 1992.

S. Mark Heim, 'The Pluralistic Hypothesis, Realism, and Post-Eschatology', *Religious Studies*, Vol. 28, no. 2 (June 1992).

Patrick Shaw, 'On Worshipping the Same God', *Religious Studies*, Vol. 28, no. 4 (December 1992).

Paul R. Eddy, 'John Hick's Theological Pilgrimage', *Proceedings of Wheaton Theology Conference* (Spring 1992).

R. Douglas Geivett, 'John Hick's Approach to Religious Pluralism', *Proceedings of Wheaton Theology Conference* (Spring 1992).

Gavin D'Costa, 'An Examination of John Hick and Paul Knitter's Theology of Religions', *Studia Missionalia*, Vol. 42 (1993).

Ian Markham, 'Creating Options: Shattering the "Exclusivist, Inclusivist, and Pluralist" Paradigm', *New Blackfriars*, Vol. 74, no. 867 (January 1993).

Harry L. Wells, 'Taking Pluralism Seriously: the Role of Metaphorical

Theology Within Interreligious Dialogue', *Journal of Ecumenical Studies*, Vol. 30, no. 1 (1993).

Philip L. Quinn, 'Religious Pluralism and Religious Relativism', *Scottish Journal of Religious Studies*, Vol. 15, no. 2 (Autumn 1994).

Robert Cook, 'Postmodernism, Pluralism and John Hick', *Themelios*, Vol. 19, no.1 (October 1993). [Reply: 'Response to Robert Cook', Vol. 19, no. 3 (May 1994).]

Dirk J. Louw, 'Theocentism and Reality-centism: a Critique of John Hick and Wilfred Cantwell Smith's Philosophy of Religious Pluralism', *South African Journal of Philosophy*, Vol. 13, no. 1 (February 1994).

S. Mark Heim, 'Salvations', *Modern Theology*, Vol. 10, no. 4 (October 1994).

Paul R. Eddy, 'Religious Pluralism and the Divine: Another Look at John Hick's Neo-Kantian Proposal', *Religious Studies*, Vol. 30, no. 4 (December 1994). [Reply: 'Religious Pluralism and the Divine: a Response to Paul Eddy', forthcoming, December 1995.]

D. J. Louw, 'The Soteriocentrism of John Hick', *South African Journal of Philosophy*, Vol. 14, no. 1 (February 1995).

## Doctoral dissertations

Noel K. Jason, 'A Critical Examination of the Christology of John Hick' (University of Sheffield, UK 1978).

Gregory Carruthers, SJ, 'The Uniqueness of Jesus Christ in the Theocentric Model of the Christian Theology of World Religions: An Elaboration and Evaluation of the Position of John Hick' (Pontifical Gregorian University, Rome 1988).*

Gerard Loughlin, 'Mirroring God's World: A Critique of John Hick's Speculative Theology' (University of Cambridge 1986).

Gavin D'Costa, 'John Hick's Theology of Religions' (University of Cambridge 1986).*

Chester Gillis, 'A Question of Final Belief: A Critical Study of the Soteriology of John Hick' (University of Chicago 1986).*

Timothy Ray Stinnett, 'The Challenge of Pluralism: A Study in the Thought of John Hick' (Southern Methodist University 1987).

Kenneth Rose, 'Knowing the Real: John Hick on the Cognitivity of Religions and Religious Pluralism' (Harvard University 1992).

## Masters' theses

Winnie Tomm, 'A Christian Approach to the World Religions: A Critical Study of Aspects of John Hick's Theology' (University of Birmingham 1980).

*published

S. E. Henshal, 'Christian Theology in the Face of Religious Pluralism' (University of Birmingham 1989).

Emi Mase, 'An Examination of John Hick's Philosophy of Religious Pluralism' (University of Bristol 1994).

Andre Albert Gerth, 'Theologie im Angesicht der Religionen: Eine Diskussion der Kritik Gavin D'Costas an der pluralistichen Religionstheologie John Hicks' (Lizentiatsarbert, Catholic Theological Faculty, University of Munich 1994).

# Index

Note: This Index does not include such terms as Christianity, Islam, Judaism, Hinduism, Buddhism, which appear very frequently, or the authors' names in Appendix II except when these are quoted in the main text.